RALPH FITCH

England's Pioneer to India and Burma

RALPH FITCH

England's Pioneer to India and Burma

HIS COMPANIONS AND CONTEMPORARIES

WITH HIS REMARKABLE NARRATIVE TOLD IN HIS OWN WORDS ÷ ÷

BY

J. HORTON RYLEY

Member of the Hakluyt Society

GYAN

Published by

Gyan Publishing House
5, Ansari Road
Daryaganj, New Delhi-110002
Phone: 011-47034999, 9811692060
E-mail: books@gyanbooks.com

Distribution Network
gyanbooks.com
India, USA, Canada, UK, Australia, France

ISBN : 978-81-212-3349-1 (PB)
First Published, London, 1899

2nd Impression 2020

Printed at: Gyan Press, Delhi.

Ralph Fitch
Author: J. Horton Ryley

RALPH FITCH

England's Pioneer to India and Burma

HIS COMPANIONS AND
CONTEMPORARIES

WITH HIS REMARKABLE NARRATIVE
TOLD IN HIS OWN WORDS + +

BY

J. HORTON RYLEY

Member of the Hakluyt Society

LONDON
T. FISHER UNWIN
PATERNOSTER SQUARE
1899

QUEEN
ELIZABETH
AND HER
COUNSELLORS

PREFACE

SO much has been written of recent years of the history of what is generally known as the East India Company, and so much interesting matter has of late been brought to light from its earliest records, that it seems strange that the first successful English expedition to discover the Indian trade should have been, comparatively speaking, overlooked. Before the first East India Company was formed the Levant Company lived and flourished, largely through the efforts of two London citizens, Sir Edward Osborne, sometime Lord Mayor, and Master Richard Staper, merchant. To these men and their colleagues we owe the inception of our great Eastern enterprise. To the fact that among them there were those who were daring enough, and intelligent enough, to carry their extraordinary programme into effect we owe our appearance as competitors in the Indian seas almost simultaneously with the Dutch. The beginning of our trade with the East Indies is generally dated from the first voyage of James Lancaster, who sailed from Plymouth in 1591. But, great as his achievement was, and immediately pregnant with consequences of a permanent character, he was not the first Englishman to reach India, nor even the first to return with a valuable store of commercial information. To keep to the chronological order of events, the Rev. Thomas Stevens, S.J., went out in 1579 to join the Jesuit establishment founded at Goa under the Portuguese, doubled the Cape of Good Hope, and ended his days in the neighbourhood of the Indian settlement. The honour of "Pioneer Englishman," however, justly belongs to Ralph Fitch, who, as the survivor of a small party of men who carried with them Royal missives to India and China, returned with some practical, if not diplomatic, results of the mission. Sailing from the Thames on board the historic ship *Tyger*, in 1583, and arriving in India as the prisoner of the united crowns of Portugal and Spain, Fitch eventually crossed the Peninsula, pursued his investigations to Burma and Malacca, and, after spending some time in Asia Minor, returned home within a month of Lancaster's first departure.

The wide public interest in the world's pioneer voyagers and empire builders—to make no further reference to the literature of the subject, more or less cognate—has been sufficiently exemplified during the last two years. France, in 1897, celebrated the two hundredth anniversary of the birth of Dupleix, as "the Conqueror of India"; in April, 1898, Florence was *en fête* in honour of the fifth centenary of Paolo Toscanelli and Amerigo Vespucci; the four hundredth anniversary of the passage of the Cape by Vasco da Gama was commemorated in May, both in

London and Lisbon; and in September, the four hundredth anniversary of the discovery of North America was marked by the opening of a tower erected at Bristol in memory of John and Sebastian Cabot. Under these circumstances it is remarkable that the story of Ralph Fitch, embodying as it does, the first English account of the great resources of India and the Further East, should have escaped adequate attention. Passing references to his adventurous journey are made by all the modern authorities; Professor Monier Williams, in the *Contemporary Review* of April, 1878, writing of the narrative and, assumedly, of the letters sent home by Fitch and his companions, says, "The account they published of their travels (preserved by Hakluyt) would well repay republication in a modern form, especially if illustrated and annotated like Colonel Yule's 'Marco Polo.'" The account of the voyage is here presented in full, with one small excision, which is duly indicated, for the first time since Hakluyt gave it to the world three centuries ago.

Whether the ideal set forth above has even been approached in this work the reader must judge; the writer puts forward no claim in regard to it, except that which may be founded on the love of his task. The plan of the book has been to introduce the account of the arduous journey by an historical summary, drawn from authoritative sources, designed to illustrate the circumstances under which it was entered upon; to borrow every additional light obtainable, either from the letters of Fitch and his companions, or the statements of those who came in contact with them ; to furnish a series of pen-portraits of the men concerned ; and, finally, to give a very brief account of the preliminary proceedings of the first East India Company, in which Ralph Fitch himself took no small part. Some deviation from this procedure occurs in reference to Burma, the most interesting British possession in the East and one which, without any doubt, will occupy a most conspicuous place in the history of the future. The notes and references, the author ventures to suggest, have not been unduly amplified, the object of this book being less to offer aid to the student than to present a popular and yet reliable account of a somewhat obscure, though fundamental, phase in the history of England's expansion.

Lord Curzon of Kedleston, Viceroy of India, has described the origin of our power in that empire in a single sentence. In an eloquent sympathic speech, delivered at a farewell banquet given to him by the Royal Societies' Club on November 7, 1898, he said that, "The casual stone which was thrown into the sea of chance by a handful of merchant adventurers two hundred years ago had produced an ever-extending circle of ripples, until at the present moment they embraced the limits and affected the destinies of the entire Asiatic continent." The story of the handful of men, and of the "casual stone," is told in the following pages, but it has been necessary to add a century and more to his lordship's retrospect.

The author has many grateful acknowledgments to make for the generous, and in some cases spontaneous, assistance rendered him during the progress of his undertaking. First, to Mr. William Foster, B.A., of the India Office, Hon. Secretary of the Hakluyt Society, for numerous most valuable suggestions, and for advice readily and freely given; also to the President and Council of the Society for permission to copy several of the rare illustrations contained in their various publications, which was most cordially granted. To Sir Owen Roberts, D.C.L., who placed the resources of the Clothworkers' Hall at his disposal; the Rev. J. A. L. Airey, M.A., Rector of St. Helen's, Bishopsgate; the Rev. A. Keble White, M.A., Rector of Great Saxham, Suffolk; Mr. W. Griggs, publisher of the *Journal of Indian Art and Industry*, "The Rulers of India and Chiefs of Rajputana," and many other luxurious works in relation to our great Empire; Mr. S. Colvin, M.A., of the Print Room, British Museum; and the officials of the British Museum Reading Room, the Record Office, and the Guildhall Library, whose willingness to assist the literary inquirer is beyond all praise. The engravings in the Museum were photographed, by permission, by Mr. Dossetter, of Acton; Messrs. Walker and Boutall, of Clifford's Inn, kindly consented to the reproduction of their photograph of Coello's fine painting of Philip II. in the National Portrait Gallery; the Osborne and Staper photographs were specially taken by the London Stereoscopic Company; and that of the Eldred bust was furnished by Mr. Spanton, of Bury St. Edmunds. References to the various works drawn upon for information will be found in the footnotes and, generally, in the body of the volume, but particular mention is due to Hakluyt's "Principall Navigations," 1599-1600, which is the foundation of this book, Sir W. W. Hunter's "Imperial Gazetteer of India," and to Sir Arthur Phayre's small but unique "History of Burma."

London, 1899.

CONTENTS

BOOK I.

BEGINNINGS OF ENGLAND'S EXPANSION.

CHAPTER I.

POLITICS, RELIGION, FREEDOM AND TRADE, 1570–83.

CHAPTER II.

ADVENTURE AND DISCOVERY.

BOOK II.

ENGLAND'S PIONEERS TO INDIA.

BOOK III.

IN THE FURTHER EAST.

CHAPTER I

CHAPTER II.

CHAPTER III.

BOOK IV.

BIOGRAPHIES, SIDELIGHTS, AND CONCLUSIONS.

ILLUSTRATIONS

BOOK I

BEGINNINGS OF ENGLAND'S EXPANSION

CHAPTER I

POLITICS, RELIGION, FREEDOM, AND TRADE (1570–83)

THE story of the perilous adventures of Master Ralph Fitch, "Marchant of London," in his endeavour to open up the Golden East to his countrymen, is in an eminent degree typical of the period, and of the Elizabethan Englishman. But in order to grasp the full meaning of the narrative, to realise the dangers of the journey, and to appreciate the great service thus rendered to this country, it is necessary to give a brief sketch of affairs as they appeared at home immediately before its commencement. For this purpose the Excommunication Year has been taken as marking a distinct departure in the policy of England and the sentiments of the people. At the same time, too much importance should not be attached to the issue of the Bull as regards its relations to English travellers abroad. There were two parties in this country when Fitch began his journey, and even in Spain and the Spanish possessions there was some sympathy, however small, for co-religionists who were supposed to desire the overthrow of the

Heretic Queen. Probably Ralph Fitch and his companions, whether they were all Roman Catholics or not, were not unwilling to be considered members of that communion till they were safe beyond the reach of Spaniard and Portuguese. But although news spread slowly in those days, the effect of the Papal anathema was practically instantaneous in Europe. In England itself it served as an incentive; it fired the spirit of independence which had already surprised surrounding nations.

Excommunication. Its effects.

So far as it is possible to reduce the foreign policy of Elizabeth, as a whole, to any definite plan, it may be described in the political language of the present day as both opportunist and adventurous. Moreover, we cannot separate—even in the imaginary fashion now in vogue—the direction of her foreign affairs from her domestic policy. Religion was the dividing force of the two great parties at home, and at the same time dominated every transaction with foreign Powers. To begin with, the Queen's title to the crown she was now wearing had been called into question by the titular head of Christendom (Paul IV.), one of whose predecessors (Alexander VI.) had shared the wonderful new worlds, East and West, between the Kings of Portugal and Spain. It only required the Bull of Excommunication of Pius V. to define the position of England, to herself as well as to the rest of Europe, as a distinct politico-religious Power—the stronghold of Protestantism, the home and starting-place of a new and more daring order of adventurers, who cared no more for Papal edicts and bans abroad than they feared the strange seas they were so well fitted to navigate. The language of the Bull was sufficiently contemptuous and provocative. Von Ranke says: "In the name of Him who had raised him to the supreme throne of Right, he (the Pope) declared Elizabeth to have forfeited the realm of which she claimed to be Queen; he not merely released her subjects from the oath they had taken to her, 'we likewise forbid,' he adds, 'her barons and peoples henceforth to obey this woman's commands and laws, under pain of excommunication.'" The personality of the author of the ban is thus described: "Pope Pius V., Michele Ghislieri, had been a Dominican inquisitor before his election to the Papacy. Austere, zealous, and determined, he devoted all his energies to the suppression of heresy. Under his rule the Inquisition crushed out Protestantism in Italy. Though a man of fervent piety and blameless life, he shrank from no measures which were likely to put down the schism. He rejoiced over Alva's cruelties in the Netherlands, and sent him a sword and cap which he had blessed, as a token of his favour."[1] With regard to the gift to the Duke of Alva, whose tortures and mutilations amongst the Protestants of the Low Countries drenched that unhappy land in blood for seven long years, Motley says his Holiness sent an autograph letter in which the recipient was requested "to remember, when he put the hat upon his head, that he was guarded with it as with a helmet of righteousness, and with the shield

[1] Dr. Creighton (Bishop of London) in "Age of Elizabeth," p. 105.

of God's help, indicating the heavenly crown which was ready for all princes who support the Holy Church and the Roman Catholic faith." [1]

The Bull and the reply.

The Bull was issued on February 25, 1570. "Several copies were sent to the Duke of Alva, with a request that he would make them known in the seaports of the Netherlands; and by the Duke some of these were forwarded to the Spanish ambassador in England. Early in the morning of the fifteenth of May, one was seen affixed to the gates of the bishop of London's residence in the capital. The Council was surprised and irritated; a rigorous search was made through the Inns of law; and another copy of the Bull was found in the chamber of a student in Lincoln's Inn, who acknowledged, on the rack, that he had received it from a person of the name of Felton. Felton resided near Southwark, a gentleman of large property and considerable acquirements: but his temper was ungovernable, and his attachment to the creed of his fathers approached to enthusiasm. On his apprehension he boldly confessed that he had set up the Bull." Lingard adds that Felton "refused, even under torture, to disclose the names of his accomplices, and abettors," but points out that the Government account of the execution, as preserved in Howell's "State Trials," represents him as repenting. Felton, it appears, "obtained the copies of the Bull from the chaplain of the Spanish ambassador, who immediately left the kingdom."

The Papal denunciation was warmly resented both

[1] "Rise of the Dutch Republic," vol. ii. p. 243.

by sovereign and people, and in the complicated condition of affairs abroad there seems to have been some doubt at first whether to regard the document as merely an act of spiritual aggression or a declaration of war by one or both of those eminently Catholic countries, Spain and France. Cecil (Lord Burleigh)—the statesman to whom, with Sir Nicholas Bacon (father of the great Francis) and Sir Francis Walsingham (the Puritan), England owed at that time so much, and still owes—fulminated a reply which by the vigour of its terms must have considerably astonished the Papal party. The manifesto is preserved in the original at the Record Office (Dom., vol. lxxiii., No. 49), and consists of thirteen pages of MS. with interlinings and marginal interpolations, all in Cecil's own hand. He begins: "An Advertiseme^n^t of mete for all uses," and addresses himself to all subjects "to know their errors and by repentance to receive mercy," and lastly, "for all strangers great or small to be well informed of truth." There is a general statement to the effect that in all ages and in all countries it has been a common usage for offenders to make defence of their real designs by untruths and by colouring their deeds ("war they never so vile"), "w^h^ pretences of sōē other courses of contrary operation," in order not merely to avoid punishment or blame but that they might prosecute their "malechoos purposes." He deals with the plottings against the Queen, "styrred upp by ye Devill ye father of rebells," and says that some have been punished and others pardoned, while special mention is made, amongst others, of Thomas Stukley, "a faythless best rather than a man." Cecil suggests that the "Bishop of Rome" was urged by these men to publish the Bull, and thus sow the seeds of sedition; he challenges the Pope's authority on historical and other grounds, and concludes "by God's grace no collor nor occasion shall be given to shed the blood of any of the Queen's subiects."[1] The fleet in the Channel was immediately reinforced, and Lord Clinton, who was in command, was instructed to attack without question any French transports he might meet taking troops to Scotland. The following year Parliament passed Bills to secure Conformity from Catholic and Puritan alike (the arbitrary Court of High Commission was made permanent in 1583), declaring it high treason to call the Queen a heretic, or to publish a Papal Bull. The natural result of the new crisis was to elevate Elizabeth to the position of the Protestant champion, an honour, be it observed, which was forced upon her, but which was soon to be emphasised by the whole course of events on the Continent, including the massacre of Bartholomew's Day (1572) and the Spanish Fury at Antwerp (1576). Still she did not venture to take up the cause of the Netherlanders or the Huguenots. Her hands were too full of the plottings at home—the Pope's message had been accompanied by letters of encouragement to the Earls of Westmorland and Northumberland—and the troubles in Scotland. So long as Spain was engaged

[1] Sir T. Stukley, the "Marqués of Ireland," was killed in 1578 whilst serving under Sebastian, King of Portugal, in an expedition to Barbary. The adventurer was in command of an Italian contingent sent by the Pope (Hakluyt, vol. ii. part ii.).

FROM AN OLD ENGRAVING MARKED "DUTCH."

in pouring the treasures of the Indies into the dykes and dunes of the Low Countries, so long as France was the scene of the varying fortunes of Huguenot and Leaguer, she felt comparatively safe, at any rate from temporal interference.

Plot and counterplot.

The Queen throughout the period under review was personally in a perilous position, and the story of the Ridolfi conspiracy, in which the most powerful monarch in Europe lent himself to a scheme for the assassination of a sovereign with whom he was in diplomatic relations, is sufficiently characteristic of the general position of affairs.[1] But she extended her sympathy to her co-religionists abroad ; although she gave them no systematic material assistance, resisting even the touching appeals of William the Silent, there was an asylum offered to the refugees in this country. Elizabeth lived in an atmosphere of plot and counterplot, and did not hesitate to stake in the game the prospect of marriage and a share of her throne. She trifled with one foreign prince or party or the other in order to secure her own inviolability, for, turn where she would, she found no country willing enough to defy the Pope, or which was not more or less under the influence of her great enemy and rival, Spain. Whilst her enemies were busy conspiring, she dallied with the Duke of Ānjou and the repulsive Alençon ("the Frog"); whilst the adventurous charlatan Sir Thomas Stukley (referred to in Cecil's manifesto), was scheming at Madrid

[1] Motley gives extracts from Philip's correspondence with Alva on the subject. Vol. ii. p. 286.

for the conquest of Ireland, the redoubtable Hawkins, in 1571, actually succeeded in so befooling Philip with offers to betray his country and his queen that the king handed over two months' pay for 1,600 men, who were to man a fleet to co-operate with Alva in an effort to place Mary of Scots on the throne of England. Froude suggests that the principal object that Hawkins had in view was to save the remnants of his force captured by the Spaniards after the treachery of San Juan de Ulloa. Such of the wretches who did not perish in Mexico, or fall victims to the Inquisition, now lay in Spanish dungeons, and Sir John, in negotiating for their release, found a daring and astute agent in one Fitzwilliam. This man carried messages between Philip and Mary of Scots, all of which were carefully inspected by Cecil *en route ;* he obtained the order for the payment of the sum mentioned above, and a "free pardon" for Hawkins, who was made a grandee of Spain for his "treachery." Another of the striking incidents of this exciting time, which may be referred to in passing, was the capture of Dr. Story, an arch-conspirator, who had sought refuge at Antwerp. A spy was sent over and induced the doctor to come aboard an English ship lying in the Scheldt. He was at once thrown into the hold, and his captor was similarly treated on the pretence that he was his fellow-prisoner, and in the hope that he might retain the doctor's confidence and obtain information from him. The Public Records contain a piteous complaint by Dr. Story, who was executed, that the irons he wore galled his legs.

The popularity, generally speaking, of Tudor government has been much discussed. In the present case there can be no question that loyalty to the queen, and to her cause as they understood it, deepened amongst the people as the reign lengthened. With regard to the condition of religion in the country, it is always difficult to gauge a national faith, and in this reign it is impossible to dissociate, on the one hand, the Papacy from the foreign element; or, on the other, Patriotism from Protestantism. In an effort to arrive at some estimate of the forces of the two great religious sects, Macaulay quotes several historians, including Lingard and Hallam. The result he reaches is that the bulk of the people, while holding firmly to the doctrines which were common to both sections, had no fixed opinion upon the matters in dispute. This conclusion he strengthens by reference to the drama of the reign; he adds, however, that the people "disliked the policy of the Court of Rome. Their spirit rose against the interference of a foreign priest with their national concerns."[1] Froude says, "Walsingham believed that at this time (1579) the establishment of the succession in a Protestant would extinguish the extreme Catholic party altogether; 'the most part of the Papists of this realm being rather of State than of conscience, in respect of the hope they have of the succession.'" Dr. Creighton remarks: "Opposition to the papacy was shown to be a necessary safeguard of the national independence.

[1] Essay on "Burleigh and His Times."

The stirring events of Elizabeth's reign bound her people together, and demanded that they should offer a united front to their foes." One of our most popular authors, who may claim the metropolis as his own peculiar ground, suggests that the only way to get at the people of the time is through those who wrote about them; behind the poets and dramatists, who were the chief glory of this age, "were the turbulent youth, prodigal of life, eager for joy, delighting in feast and song, always ready for a fight, extravagant in speech and thought, jubilant in their freedom from the tyranny of the Church." He further states: "If the London of the Third Edward was a city of palaces, that of Queen Elizabeth was a city of ruins," and adds, in effect, that the appropriation or destruction of many Catholic establishments was witnessed with indifference.[1]

Commerce and industry.

"When Queen Elizabeth ascended the throne, the commercial centre of the world was Antwerp; when she died the commercial centre of the world was London."[2] Thus writes one authority. Another says: "The reign of Elizabeth is the epoch from which dates the naval and commercial greatness of England, and the queen's care and attention contributed in no slight degree to this result."[3] We have here, as it were, the conception and realisation of a brilliant vision placed in juxtaposition. But what comes between? It is impossible to peruse the most dramatic page of England's history without

[1] Sir Walter Besant in "London."

[2] Sir W. Besant. [3] Dr. Creighton.

being almost overpowered by a sense of Opportunity. The programme of Elizabeth and her courageous Ministers from the beginning was one of freedom, first from the power of the Pope. But to all intents and purposes this meant isolation. The English became the Ishmaelites of Europe, with enemies whose resources were only outnumbered by their vulnerable points. The defensive struggle for religious freedom soon developed into a contest for Commercial Equality and subsequently—as the courage which prompted the first defiance of Catholic Europe became more and more daring—into an aggressive spirit of Expansion.[1] The conditions under which the world's trade was carried on were peculiarly favourable to the enterprise, and with a prescience which, looked at from a distance, appears altogether remarkable, the queen prepared for coming events in a substantial, honest manner. One of the first acts of her reign was the restoration of the coinage, which had been debased to one-third of its face value. The worst debasements were made by Henry VIII. and Edward VI., so that in 1551 no less than seventy-two shillings were coined out of a pound. A thorough change was made by Elizabeth,

[1] Prof. Seeley in his collected lectures on the "Expansion of England" deals in a searching manner with the revolutionary influences of the Reformation and the discovery of the New World—influences which made themselves felt within thirty years of each other. The former, he holds, was the more rapid in its operation on the Old World, but the effects died sooner than those of the latter; it was not till near the end of the sixteenth century, after the repeated raids upon the Spanish settlements in Central America, that Spain decided upon her great enterprise against England.

who coined only sixty shillings at first out of a pound of silver; but afterwards in 1601 she coined sixty-two shillings, and so it remained till 1816, when sixty-six shillings were coined.[1] But apart from the semi-political and romantic schemes which are referred to below, the whole of her commercial policy was directed to the encouragement of the native merchant at the expense, it might be, of his foreign rivals. Those were the days of Merchant Guilds, and it is an open question whether the England of the present day does not owe quite as much to the energy and enterprise of the traders of that age as to its politicians and explorers; "trade follows the flag" is now a trite saying, but it did not apply under Elizabeth.

Merchant princes.

At the head of all the European guilds was the great Hanseatic League. The League, whose history is a veritable romance of commerce, negotiated with monarchs and threatened princes.[2] The chief depôt in England was in London, and the mercantile colony, enclosed in walls and gates, came to be known as the Steelyard, probably from the fact that on this spot stood the great balance of the city, on which all imported and exported merchandise had to be officially weighed. The great power and widespread influence of the Hansards, as they were called, who appear to have first sprung into prominence in the northern seas

[1] Gibbins's "History of Commerce in Europe" (Macmillan, 1891).

[2] For a history of the great Hanseatic League, probably unique in its completeness, see Helen Zimmern's "The Hansa Towns" (Story of the Nations Series. Fisher Unwin).

about the end of the twelfth century, may be traced on a map which shows that in the middle of the sixteenth century their depôts and possessions extended from London to Novgorod, and from Bergen to Krakow. Their privileges were systematically attacked in this country in the reign of Edward VI., but they recovered their entire liberties under Mary. All this was changed under Elizabeth, by the labours of Cecil and Sir Thomas Gresham, financier and merchant. In 1597 the Emperor Rudolph, much to the delight of the Hansards in their headquarters at Lübeck, ordered all English traders to leave the empire within three months. In reply Elizabeth gave the League notice to quit the Steelyard within fourteen days, a mandate which the Mayor and Sheriffs saw duly carried out; but eventually the property was restored to the Germans minus the trade privileges. It is interesting to add that as late as 1853 the Steelyard was sold to an English company for building purposes, for the sum of £72,500, by the cities of Lübeck, Bremen, and Hamburg, and the present Cannon Street railway station stands on part of the site.

On the suppression of these foreign monopolists home-made combinations sprung into life and flourished amazingly, and particular mention may be made of the development of the guilds of the Merchants of the Staple and the Merchant Adventurers. Both seem to have arisen towards the end of the thirteenth century—the Staplers first—and were known under the same title of the Brotherhood of St. Thomas à Becket. Most of their business was in manufactured cloth, and they were probably offshoots of the Company of Mercers, whose patron saint was the same. They established "staples" or depôts abroad, and it is stated that in 1550 the Adventurers employed no less than 20,000 persons at Antwerp alone, and 30,000 elsewhere in the Netherlands. In 1568 Alva seized their merchandise at Antwerp, and Elizabeth promptly retaliated on the Spanish shipping. It is not difficult to understand that both bodies were in constant conflict, at home and abroad, with the Hanseatic League. The Adventurers were invited to Bruges during the Spanish troubles, but they replied that "until religious freedom is granted and taxation reduced it is impossible;" they finally settled at Hamburg till their work in the world was done. The Corporation of Staplers continued till the eighteenth century and held meetings, though their trade and importance had long since passed away.[1] "At the beginning of the reign," writes Sir Walter Besant, "there were no more than 317 merchants in all, of whom the Company of Mercers formed 96. Before her reign it was next to impossible for the city to raise a loan of £10,000. Before she died the city was advancing to the Queen loans of £60,000." "In 1572," says Froude, "the burden of all vessels in the kingdom which were

[1] An historical account of these earlier English trade guilds is given in "Two Thousand Years of Gild Life," by the Rev. J. Malet Lambert, M.A. (Simpkin, Marshall, 1891). See also "The Early Chartered Companies," by Messrs. George Cawston and A. H. Keene, F.R.G.S. (Edward Arnold, 1896), in which the origin of Staple Inn, Holborn, is traced to the merchant company of that name.

engaged in ordinary commerce scarcely exceeded 50,000 tons" (actual 50,926 tons), while the largest sailing vessel from the port of London was of only 240 tons burden.

An epoch in the history of English commerce was the opening of the first London Royal Exchange by the Queen in 1571, a "bourse" after the fashion of that at Antwerp, which was presented to the City by Sir Thomas Gresham. So much has been said and written of this typical London merchant—typical, that is, of his time—that little need be added here. His official relations as financial agent or broker of the English Government at home and abroad continued off and on from 1553 to 1574, and were concluded in a manner which bears testimony to his ingenuity, to say nothing more. The Commissioners of the Treasury, it appears, made some startling discoveries in the details of his final account and docked a variety of counter claims. But Gresham was equal to the emergency. He paid a visit to the official auditor, who was on the point of going for his summer holiday, and solicited a copy of the official account on the plea that all his own papers had been lodged with the authentic account. This was supplied, and the official left for his vacation. "Immediately Gresham caused the usual concessary footnote to be added to this imperfect document, setting forth the statement and allowance of his claim for interest and exchange on the surplus, already rejected, and posted off to Kenilworth, where the Queen was now being royally entertained by Leicester." By some means he gained the royal sanction for this copy, and armed with such authority he obtained the signatures of the Commissioners, who were apparently in attendance at Court. When the astonished auditor was presented with his own duplicate, signed and with footnote complete, he was compelled to treat it as the authoritative record, though it involved the disposition of six millions (present value).[1] But on the whole it is difficult to estimate the services of this man to his day and generation. He fought the battle of the native merchants against the Hansards, and kept the State Loans in the country; by his means a mart, destined to become the greatest in the world, was established here.

Industrial refugees. Meanwhile a series of circumstances had been in operation which, whilst illustrating the permeating influences of the rival religions of the time, reveals another of the beginnings of England's industrial as well as commercial greatness. Up to the accession of Elizabeth our most important export had been home-grown wool, which went to the manufacturers of Flanders. But during the growing uneasiness consequent upon the policy of Philip in the Low Countries emigration had set in, chiefly, of course, to England. In 1566 matters reached a climax, and the famous Compromise was presented to the Regent, the Duchess Margaret, as

[1] From "Society in the Elizabethan Age," by Mr. Hubert Hall of the Record Office. "It is not too much to say," continues Mr. Hall, "that Gresham was £10,000 (£60,000) to the good by the successful issue of his mission. He had received this sum, and had not accounted for it. . . . In sober truth, however, Gresham was neither better nor worse than the age made him."

a protest against the Spanish Inquisition. By this time it is computed that no less than 50,000 wretched Netherlanders had been put to death under Philip's edicts, while 30,000 had left the country and settled at Norwich, Sandwich, and other places. Elizabeth, with her usual shrewdness—to suggest no higher motive—gave all these expert artisans a cordial welcome, but made it a condition that each industrial house should employ at least one English apprentice. The refugees and the English lads between them soon established such a cloth and silk making and dyeing business as to completely turn the tide of trade. Instead of the raw material going to the Scheldt to come back in the shape of manufactured goods, they sent the finished article.

How much the spirit of Protestantism in England owed eventually to these circumstances it would be impossible to estimate. Froude suggests, by way of accounting for the strange admixture of religion and marauding, persecution and piracy, witnessed in the English Channel and elsewhere during a nominal time of peace between England and Spain, that the ideas of the Reformation had taken the deepest root amongst the sea-going portion of Elizabeth's subjects. But there can be no question that a generous sympathy with the industrious Netherland refugees, coupled with the hatred of the power which was felt to be the common enemy, spread rapidly among the increasing artisan class in this country, and, ascending higher in the social scale, reached the merchant and the courtier, not to say the Queen herself. "The merchant," says the historian just quoted, "therefore could change his character for that of buccaneer with the approval of his conscience as well as to the advantage of his purse. When driven from legitimate trade the English merchants, instead of flying at the Government as the Spanish ambassador had hoped, flew upon the spoils of those who forced them to abandon it." Thus Philip's policy, carried out as it was in the Low Countries with all the ferocity of Alva, and perfectly understood, especially so far as the plottings were concerned, by Cecil and Walsingham, was made in the long run to recoil upon itself.

PORTRAIT OF THE TSAR IVAN (IV.) VASILIVITCH.

CHAPTER II

ADVENTURE AND DISCOVERY

IN endeavouring to realise something of the commencement of England's dominion over the sea before the fatal blow had been struck at the greatest existing ocean power, in the defeat of the Spanish Armada (1588), we encounter a set of circumstances which it is difficult to understand in these days. The reaction from the Papal Bull accounts for much of the predatory spirit of the English at this time; although we were not at war with any country in Europe, the Channel swarmed with freebooters, who found a ready refuge on our coasts. The "Water Beggars" of the Netherlands, under Brederode, and the wild and savage William de la Marck harried the Spaniards with conspicuous impunity. In the spring of 1571 their fleet came into Dover Roads and, being joined by several English rovers, they held the Straits, raided the Spanish coasts, and plundered the king's ships. Markets were held at Dover, where the proceeds of

Pirates and the Royal Navy.

the operations were openly disposed of and captives were sold for the ransom they would bring, being actually consigned to the court-house in irons.[1] When Alva sent a squadron to rid the Channel of these hornets Brederode drew in under the cliffs, and the English batteries beat off the Spaniards. In reply to a protest, the Spanish ambassador was informed that "English waters were a sanctuary." In 1572, however, on a remonstrance from Alva, Elizabeth, "wishing," as Dr. Creighton puts it, "to be conciliatory in a little matter," gave orders that the "Water Beggars" should not be supplied with provisions. De la Marck thereupon set sail with his four-and-twenty ships, and his total force of not more than 250 men, and, being driven by stress of weather into the mouth of the Meuse, succeeded by a bold stroke in capturing the town of Brill for Prince William of Orange.

This was the period of renaissance for the Royal Navy, in which the Queen from the first exhibited the liveliest interest, though her subsequent niggardliness imperilled the safety of her realm. At the death of Henry VIII. the navy consisted of 53 vessels, with an aggregate burden of 6,255 tons, and a total complement—officers, soldiers, sailors, and gunners—of about 8,000 men. The largest vessel was the *Great Harry* of 1,000 tons. At the death of Edward VI. the number of ships had come down to 45, of which only 24 were effective. Matters became worse under Mary, and almost at the commencement of her reign the *Great Harry* was burnt at Woolwich "by the

[1] Froude.

negligence of the mariners."[1] Miserably depleted as it had been during the two previous reigns, Elizabeth followed a systematic plan of restoring the arm to a nucleus of effective strength, and at the period under notice she had a small but well-formed force to cruise around the coasts. The fleet was not large enough, however, to maintain peace in the Channel, so far as English subjects were concerned, even if this had been the consistent intention of the Government; indeed on more than one occasion royal ships were actually allowed to be used for very different purposes. By 1578 she had succeeded in forming a fleet of 24 vessels, with a total complement of 7,000 men, the largest being the *Triumph*, 1,000 tons, while there were two of 900 tons, two of 800 tons, five of 600 tons and so on down to 60 tons. The redoubtable Sir John Hawkins—who, although there is some suspicion of his financial practices, was at least a practical seaman—succeeded his father-in-law, Gonson, as Comptroller, and Sir William Winter was the Master of Naval Ordnance. Meanwhile enterprise and adventure had been carried on far beyond these shores, till at last the fortitude, endurance, and courage displayed in various parts of the globe opened out permanent avenues to commerce, and laid the foundations of the British Empire.

It need not be a matter of surprise that the beginnings of expansion were left to individual adventurers and small combinations of merchants—surely such a

[1] See Mr. Fox Bourne's "English Seamen under the Tudors" for these figures and a graphic account of the maritime history of the period (Bentley, 1868).

commencement should be rather a matter of congratulation than otherwise. Troubled with the most complicated affairs of State, the Queen could do little more than watch with a kindly eye, and sanction by charter and missive, the efforts of her subjects in distant regions. At first she was cautious in what she did sanction, and the records afford ample evidence that the more daring of her navigators found it necessary to make public explanations, more or less lame as they appear to us, of what they had done and why they had done it. But Elizabeth never forgot that she was a proscribed person, that her kingdom was in a state of incipient antagonism to the leading European Powers, and, secretly to begin with, then openly and defiantly, she furthered the projects of her vigorous, almost unruly adventurers, thus reaping a rich reward for herself and leaving a greater one for posterity. Up to the time of the departure of Master Ralph Fitch for India and the Far East (1583) various of his countrymen had within comparatively recent years penetrated to other distant lands, but a summary of their doings will suffice.[1]

[1] Mention should be made here of an attempt to reach the Far East which, although futile in its results, deserves a place as the first organised expedition in this direction. Hakluyt (vol. iii. p. 754) thus describes it: "The voyage of M. Edward Fenton and M. Luke Ward, his vice-admirall, with 4 ships, intended for China, but performed onely to the coast of Brazil as farre as 33. degrees of southerly latitude: begunne in the yeare 1582." The account is written by Ward, who was in command of the *Edward Bonaventura*, 300 tons, a sturdy ship which afterwards figured in the attack on the Spanish Armada, and carried Lancaster to India on his first voyage in 1591.

To N.E. Ivan the Terrible.

To deal first with what may be described as the purely English efforts to discover a north-east or north-west passage to Far Cathay, and without going so far back as the voyages of the Cabots, we come primarily to the setting forth of an expedition which resulted in the opening up of a seaborne trade with Russia, a result at least as important to that country as our own. The voyage is attributed to the suggestion of Sebastian Cabot, now an old man, who had returned to England from service with Spain, and it was "for the search and discovery of the northern part of the world." Sir Hugh Willoughby and Richard Chancelor, in command of three vessels, set out in 1553, the route, roughly planned, being to sail northerly as far as possible, then easterly and southward. Beyond the North Cape they became separated in a fog, and two years afterwards the remains of Willoughby and the crews of two of his ships were found in a small Lapland bay. Chancelor, being unable to discover his companions, continued the journey and found his way into the White Sea. Here he met with a hospitable reception, was invited to Moscow and, quite in modern fashion, secured a commercial treaty from Ivan the Terrible. This commencement of intercourse between two nations destined in the future—rightly or wrongly—to become rivals in the heritage of the East and Far East, is one of the most fascinating incidents of a moving epoch. Ivan IV., who was the first to assume the title of Tsar, was now twenty-three years of age, and had already demonstrated, in his own fashion, his power to rule. He granted permission to Richard Chancelor "and the guests arrived from the English land with wares brought in their ships from beyond the seas, to come and go in safety in his Russian dominions and to buy and build houses without let or hindrance." Abandoning all idea of continuing the search for the North-East passage, Chancelor returned home, and soon afterwards the relations of the two countries became sufficiently advanced to enter upon the diplomatic stage. The first Russian ambassador was sent to this country (to Mary and Philip) on the occasion of Chancelor's second voyage in 1556. The return journey, however, proved most disastrous; the English navigator and all the three ships were lost, but the ambassador was saved, and eventually entered London in state. An adventurous Englishman, one Anthony Jenkinson, visited the country in 1557 and was employed on various expeditions; he was sent back to Moscow as Elizabeth's ambassador in 1566.[1] The next voyage was undertaken in 1580, for the Muscovy Company, by Jackman and Pet. They reached the Kara Sea, the former by Burrough's Straits and the latter by the channel now known as Pet's Straits.

[1] See Prof. Morfill's "Russia" (Story of the Nations Series). The journeyings of Anthony Jenkinson will be found in Hakluyt's Collection, and also in "Early Voyages and Travels in Russia and Persia," edited for the Hakluyt Society by Messrs. E. Delmar Morgan and C. H. Coote. The earliest account of Muscovy, by Baron Sigismund von Hebrerstein, German ambassador 1517–26, has been translated and edited for the society by Mr. R. H. Major.

To N.W.; Colonisation.

About the year 1574 systematic steps were taken to revive the quest for the North-West passage. As the result of the written and other efforts of Sir Humphrey Gilbert and Martin Frobisher, the Queen wrote to the Muscovy Company, which had been formed, suggesting that if they did not intend to pursue the exploration of a northerly route to Cathay they should transfer their privileges to other adventurers. As the Company were satisfied with their profitable Russian traffic they granted a licence in 1575 to Frobisher, whose three voyages to the North-West (1575–9), after the formation of the Company of Cathay, and whose reward of a knighthood are well-known matters of history.[1] Sir Humphrey Gilbert in 1578 obtained a charter for the discovery and possession of any barbarous lands not yet claimed by a Christian prince, and he was joined, though not accompanied, in this somewhat wide venture by his stepbrother, Walter Raleigh, so soon to become famous. Gilbert, unfortunate as he was, may be fittingly described as the father of British colonisation. His first expedition, which was to found a colony somewhere in North America, left England in 1578, but was beaten back by the Spaniards, and returned in 1579. In 1583 he started again, steering for Newfoundland, where the English had for some time enjoyed a share of the fisheries, his idea being to sail southward afterwards to find a suitable spot to found a permanent

[1] The Hakluyt Society have published the three voyages in volume form, with selections from State papers, edited by Rear-Admiral Collinson, C.B.

home. He, however, fixed upon St. John's, but after a brief spell ashore, which was long enough to exhibit the inherent weakness of the whole scheme, the expedition set off on the return journey, Gilbert's vessel—he chose the smallest of his little fleet—foundering at sea.

The Spanish Main. Fight for sea supremacy.

The next portion of the moving story of storm and stress carries us through strange seas to unknown coast-lines: it tells of plundered treasure-ships; of results which established the reputation of Englishmen as the bravest—to say no more—as well as the most skilful of navigators. It has been urged, specially in reference to Drake's greatest exploit, that, in the encouragement she gave to the questionable doings of her seamen in these expeditions, Elizabeth made a most valuable contribution to the war in the Low Countries, and that it was more effective "in bringing Spain upon her knees than if she had emptied her treasury into the lap of Orange." But, whatever were the Queen's motives, there can be no doubt of the encouragement, intermittent though it seems to have been, nor of the peculiar opportunities which had been growing up for its exercise. As far back as 1530–2 William Hawkins of Plymouth, father of the more famous John, had sailed to the Guinea Coast, and appears to have been our pioneer in a trade in which Martin Frobisher and Francis Drake subsequently served their deep-sea apprenticeship. Hawkins's plan was to make a round voyage from England to Guinea, thence to Brazil—where, after Sebastian Cabot, now in the Spanish service, he was the first English representative—and then home. The Guinea route was soon pursued by others, and we find Captain Windham, under the guidance of Pinteado, a Portuguese, sailing in 1553 and trading with Benin. In 1562 John Hawkins—whose name is so unhappily associated with the slave traffic, the enormities of which, it is only fair to suggest, were not at all understood at the time—set himself to work to trade between Africa and the Spanish colonies. In 1563 he returned from San Domingo with his three English ships, sending two Spanish vessels which he had chartered to Cadiz. Here, however, Philip II., who looked upon the whole affair with jealous eyes, seized the vessels and prohibited the enterprise. For the next trading expedition to the Spanish Main, 1564, Elizabeth allowed Hawkins to hire one of her largest vessels; several of her nobles shared in the venture, which proved highly successful, and on his return the navigator was honoured with a crest and coat of arms. In 1567, in company with Drake, Hawkins set sail on the memorable voyage to the West Indies and the Mexican coast, which ended in the treachery of San Juan de Ulloa and a declaration of open enmity to Spain from the two English seamen who were destined to do probably more than any others to damage irretrievably her naval supremacy.

Soon afterwards political matters in England reached an acute stage. Froude says: "In the spring of 1571, when the Spanish ambassador had been discovered to be a party to the Norfolk conspiracy (the Ridolfi plot), a hint was given to the Western privateers, and a young adventurer sailed out of Plymouth harbour more enterprising and more audacious than the dreaded Hawkins himself." This was Drake's expedition to Nombre de Dios, and although its intention and character were well known, the Queen appears to have made no secret of her personal interest in the enterprise. The "young adventurer" returned with an enormous amount of booty from the Isthmus of Panama, and, what was of more importance, with a considerably widened view as a navigator—for he had seen the Pacific Ocean, and had come to the determination to find his way thither, and to solve the problem of the North-West passage from the other side of the North American continent. About four years afterwards Oxenham the rover crossed the isthmus, and, having built a pinnace, made prizes amongst the coasters of the Pacific which brought bullion from Lima, but he was eventually captured and hanged.[1]

Drake's circumnavigation.

Drake's next voyage, which was to hand his name down to history as the first circumnavigator, which was to dispose of the fictions designedly circulated by the sailors of Spain and Portugal concerning the almost insurmountable difficulties to be met with in the Straits of Magellan on the one hand, and on the other in the passage of the Cape of Good Hope; which was, in short, to lay the foundation of England's claim of empire over the sea, was commenced in the winter of 1577, and, again, at a crisis in the history

[1] Hakluyt gives a short account of the doings of "John Oxnam of Plimmouth," vol. iii. p. 526.

of his country. Don John of Austria, the hero of Lepanto, who had become the new governor of the Netherlands, undertook his charge with the deliberate intention of utilising his Spanish veterans for an invasion of England. The "Spanish Fury" at Antwerp in 1576, and the united demand from both Catholic and Protestants for the withdrawal of the Spanish troops from the Low Countries, seemed to further his purpose admirably. But, designedly or otherwise, probably the truth of the matter will never be known, the Netherland States insisted on the departure by land, and this was effected at the beginning of the year. Under these circumstances it need hardly be a matter of surprise that Elizabeth should have countenanced another scheme, the success of which, as she must have foreseen, could only be to the detriment of Spain. Possibly another reason for her action may be found in the mission of the Marquis of Havré from the struggling Netherlanders, who feared a *rapprochement* between Don John and the Catholics of France.

A short time before the departure of Drake a remarkable letter was sent to the Queen, which may be taken as representing the curious mixture of daring and diplomacy of the Englishmen of the time. It is dated November 6th, and in the original, which is preserved among the Domestic MSS. at the Public Record Office, the signature is erased. The writer says :—

"Your Majesty must first seek the kingdom of heaven, and make no league with those whom God has divided from you. Your Majesty must endeavour to make yourself strong and to make them weak, and at sea you can either make war on them openly or by colourable means:—by giving licence, under letters patent, to discover and inhabit strange places, with special proviso for their safeties whom policy requires to have most annoyed—by which means the doing the contrary shall be imputed to the executors' fault: your Highness's letters patent being a manifest show that it was not your Majesty's pleasure so to have it. Afterwards, if it seem well, you can avow the fact, or else you can disavow the fact and those that did it as league-breakers, leaving them to pretend it was done without your privity. I will undertake, if you will permit me, to fit out ships, well armed, for Newfoundland, where they will meet with all the great shipping of France, Spain, and Portugal. The best I will bring away and I will burn the rest. Commit us afterwards as pirates if you will, but I shall ruin their sea force, for they depend on their fishermen for their navies. It may be objected that this will be against your league; but I hold it as lawful in Christian policy to prevent a mischief betimes as to revenge it too late; especially seeing that God himself is a party to the quarrel now on foot, and His enemy maliciously disposed towards your Highness. You may be told it will ruin our commerce. Do not believe it: you will but establish your own superiority at sea. If you will let us first do this, we will next take the West Indies from Spain. You will have the gold and silver mines and the profit of the soil. You will be monarch of the seas and out of danger from everyone. I will do it if you will allow me: only you must resolve and not delay or dally—The wings of man's life are plumed with the feathers of death."

Froude, who has been quoted, further states that the fleet was "equipped by a company of adventurers, among whom the Queen and Leicester were the largest shareholders," while, as to the ostensible object of the expedition, it was "to search the waste of the Pacific and find openings for English commerce; but with private instructions from the Queen, which might be shown or withheld, acted upon or not acted upon, as convenience might afterwards dictate."

Its results.

Drake sailed in December, 1577, in command of four vessels and a pinnace, the largest ship of the squadron being the *Pelican* (afterwards called the *Golden Hind*, in honour, it is supposed, of Sir Christopher Hatton) of only 120 tons, the total complement of the fleet being 164 men. It is not necessary here to follow the navigator in detail in his ever-to-be-remembered voyage.[1] There was tragedy enough and adventure enough in all conscience. At Port St. Julian, on the Patagonian coast, Thomas Doughty, the second in command—and, it has been suggested, a secret agent of the Catholic party—was executed for mutiny and his vessel burnt. Leaving the pinnace at this "port," the *Pelican*, *Elizabeth*, and the 30-ton cutter successfully passed Magellan's Straits. Meeting violent weather on entering the Pacific the cutter was lost, and Winter in the *Elizabeth*, having lost sight of Drake, succeeded in making the return passage through the Straits, and arrived in England in June, 1578. The *Pelican*, or *Golden Hind* as the vessel was now called, with a ship's company of between eighty and ninety men, commenced a career of exploration and

[1] "The World Encompassed by Sir Francis Drake," collated with an unpublished manuscript of Francis Fletcher, chaplain to the expedition, has been edited for the Hakluyt Society by Mr. W. S. W. Vaux, M.A.

warfare which is unique in history. We have given one reference to the records of the voyage, others may be found in Hakluyt's collection and in the State papers. Apart from the financial results, it is of considerable interest to note that Drake, in pursuit of the north-west passage, sailed northward to the Californian coast. He met with hospitable treatment from the natives, who saw Europeans for the first time, and took formal possession of the region, which he dubbed "New Albion." But, anxious to preserve his questionably gotten treasure, and leaving behind the snow-capped mountains of the north, he pursued his way by the Pelew and Philippine Islands, threaded the Moluccas, doubled the Cape of Good Hope, and eventually reached Plymouth in October, 1580, after an absence of two years and ten months. His arrival caused immense sensation, the results of the voyage, so far as the treasure was concerned, more than confirming the rumours that had preceded him, which were chiefly based on the reports sent across the Isthmus of Panama to Spain by the Viceroy of Callao. The queen shuffled in reply to the indignant protests of the Spanish ambassador, Mendoza, and knighted Drake.[1] Possibly the delay

[1] Various calculations have been made of the value of the tons of silver and the large sums of gold and jewels seized either ashore or afloat on the South American coast by this single vessel, which contained a mere handful of men. In the case of the plundering of the treasure-ship *Our Lady of the Conception* (the *Cacafuego* the English sailors called her) alone, the Spanish Government reckoned their loss at a million and a half of ducats (worth about 9s. 6d. each), an amount which, adds Froude, was never questioned.

in the action of Spain in reply to this deliberate attack upon the sources of her wealth abroad may be found in the fact that Philip's attention was absorbed in Portugal on the one hand, and in the Netherlands on the other. It was in 1580 that he seized upon the crown of the former country, his claim being based upon the fact that his mother was the daughter of King Manuel; Dom Antonio, a natural son of the royal house, and also a claimant, was driven out of Portugal, eventually finding an asylum in this country. In the same year Philip published his infamous Ban, which set a price upon the head of William of Orange.

Aspiration. There can be no question that Drake's circumnavigation, disposing as it did of many sailors' fictions, opened the eyes of his countrymen to the possibilities of a vast foreign trade, and at the same time exposed the weak side of the much-dreaded power of Spain. It is true, as we have to some extent shown, that there was no lack of adventurers, some of whom had met with no meagre measure of success. But Drake had sailed round the whole world, had fought the Spaniards on their own high seas, and had come back, loaded with untold wealth, to reap honours. To suggest that the Spanish Armada was launched in 1588 merely to punish these plunderings of 1577–80 would be absurd. Philip—after repeated raids on his colonies it is true—simply attacked England in her turn, and at a time most convenient to himself. But in the interval a spirit had been growing up for which he never calculated, and such men as Drake and John

Hawkins, Frobisher, Raleigh, and Gilbert were inspired by it. The love of adventure; the hope of something afar off; the stretching forth, as it were, of unshackled limbs; the drinking in of purer and unaccustomed air—these affected the whole mass of a constitutionally vigorous people, who, almost intoxicated as they were by their new-found aspirations, could approach their Sovereign with a certainty of finding sentiments peculiarly in harmony with their own; wisdom, better trained and wider than their own; courage and rough-and-ready daring, equal to their own.

In his graphic picture of the time Sir Walter Besant tells of the bronzed and scarred veterans who sat in the tavern and told, between their cups of sack, of the wonders that lay beyond the ocean, to an audience who had not yet got beyond believing in "the Ethiopian with four eyes, the Arimaspi with one eye, the Hippopodes or Centaurs, the Monopoli, or men who have no head, but carry their faces in their breasts and their eyes in their shoulders. None of these monsters, it is true, had ever been caught and brought home; but many an honest fellow, if hard pressed by his hearers, would reluctantly confess to having seen them." Of the adventurers of the humbler sort we have Miles Philips, who sailed with Hawkins to the West Indies and, after the episode of San Juan de Ulloa, was put ashore with others near Panuco in 1568. This man spent many miserable years as a prisoner of the Spaniards. His stirring story was published in 1582, and is preserved in Hakluyt's Collection (vol. iii.), along with that of a fellow-mariner, one Job Hortop. Peter Carder, the only survivor of the crew of Drake's pinnace, also returned to England after an extraordinary series of experiences in 1586, and told his tale to the Queen.

To the East Indies. These were the circumstances and these the times in which Master Ralph Fitch and his companions began their memorable journey to India and the Far East. Despite the relentless cruelties of the Spanish inquisitors, even to castaways like Philips, Englishmen could be found in any number to join any expedition even to unknown regions. But in this case a systematic attempt was to be made to study on the spot the nature of a trade which had so much enriched the two great monarchies of Spain and Portugal. The undertaking cannot be described altogether as an exploration, for the travellers mainly followed well-beaten tracks. It was mainly intended to get at the sources of a most profitable system of commerce; and whether the ultimate end was to be a diversion of some of it to the benefit of the already growing Levant trade with England, or to establish over-sea communications *viâ* the Cape—which ultimately proved to be the case—were matters probably left for consideration till after the results of the venture were made known. A superior class of man was obviously required for such an enterprise. Newberie was an experienced traveller and merchant, Fitch was eminently fitted for the task by education, native shrewdness, and the power of clear, concise description, as the reader will shortly have an opportunity of judging. Leedes and Story were at least clever tradesmen. So far as the records go, the little party had only been preceded in the journey to India by one Englishman, Stevens the Jesuit, whom they found at Goa and who had reached that emporium as early as 1579 by a different route. They began their journey at a most critical period in European history, and voluntarily placed themselves in the power of their country's most bigoted and bitter enemy, whose wrath had just been excited by the depredations of a fellow-countryman. For cool and deliberate daring the journey of Fitch and his fellow-travellers hardly finds a parallel even in Elizabethan history; its ultimate results will be found in a modern map of India.

BOOK II

ENGLAND'S PIONEERS TO INDIA

Photo] [*Walker & Boutall, London.*

PHILIP II. (COELLO).

CHAPTER I

QUEEN'S LETTERS TO INDIA AND CHINA—REMARKABLE RELATION OF RALPH FITCH—VOYAGE TO GOA—IMPRISONED

The Levant or Turkey Company.

THE setting forth of Master Ralph Fitch and his companions appears to have had its origin in the enterprise of the newly formed Levant Company, afterwards known as the Turkey Company. Records are preserved of voyages made early in the sixteenth century to various Mediterranean ports in Sicily, Crete, Cyprus, and to Tripoli and Beyrout in Syria, while we had a Consul stationed at Chios as early as 1513. In Hakluyt's Collection we find an account of the perilous voyage of the *Holy Cross* and the *Matthew Gonson* to Crete and Chios in 1534. In 1550 Captain Bodenham, in "the great Barke *Aucher*," went the same journey, and states that "Richard Chancellor, who first discovered Russia, was with me in that voyage." Three years later Anthony Jenkinson, already referred to, who was then at Aleppo, obtained "a safe conduct" from Sultan Solyman, which has been described as the actual foundation of our future capitulations and the commencement of the Levant Company. In 1579 three merchants, William Harebone (or Hareborne), Edward Ellis, and Richard Staple (apparently the Richard Staper mentioned below), were sent to Constantinople to obtain for English merchants the privileges enjoyed by other nations.[1] In 1581 Elizabeth entered into a treaty with Amurath (Murad) III. for five years, and granted letters patent to a small company entitled, "The Company of Merchants of the Levant." The charter was issued to Sir Edward Osborne, Thomas Smith, Richard Staper, and William Garret. "Her Majesty therefore grants unto those four merchants and to such other Englishmen, not exceeding twelve in number, as the said Sir E. Osborn and Staper shall appoint to be joined to them and their factors, servants, and deputies, for the space of seven years to trade to Turkey." The exclusive right

[1] "Early Voyages and Travels in the Levant," edited for the Hakluyt Society by the late Mr. J. Theodore Bent, F.S.A., F.R.G.S. The author further points out that the carrying trade between England and the Levant had hitherto been chiefly in the hands of the Venetians. Their ships were called "argosies," and Sir Paul Ricaut, some time Consul at Smyrna, gives an unexpected explanation of the name by stating that they were so called because they were built at Ragusa, *i.e.*, "Ragosies." In 1575, after one of their vessels had been wrecked on the Isle of Wight, the Venetian merchants hesitated to navigate such dangerous seas, and in the same year a dispute arose concerning duties. Still another cause which tended to promote our independent intercourse with Turkey was that Elizabeth entered upon her vital contest with Philip II.; in fact, in 1587, in view of the Armada preparations, her agent at Constantinople was actually instructed to appeal to the Sultan for aid against "the idolater the King of Spain," happily without practical result.

to trade was given on three clauses—subject to revocation on a year's notice; that the Queen might add two members to the number of patentees; and that a renewal for another seven years might be granted, provided that the said exclusive trade should not appear to be unprofitable to the kingdom. Such was the original charter, and what happened soon afterwards was distinctly characteristic of a period when the highest in the land felt, and did not hesitate to show, a warm personal interest in the development of the commerce of the country. It is recorded that in the early days of the enterprise, "the members of the association attending on the Queen and Council received great thanks and high commendation 'for the ships they then built of so great burthen,' with many encouragements also to go forward 'for the kingdom's sake.'"[1] The first vessel despatched by the new organisation of merchants was sent out in 1582. It was called the *Great Susan*, and carried William Hareborne, our first plenipotentiary (or ambassador as Hakluyt describes him) to the Sultan.

[1] "The Early Chartered Companies," *q.v.* It is hardly necessary to add that by the natural operations of time and change the Turkey Company at last entered upon a period of disintegration and decay, but it did not cease to exist till 1825. Chesney ("Survey of Euphrates and Tigris") states that Newberie and Fitch were sent out by the Company. He also refers to a petition from the Company to the Queen, given in the Cotton Collection (Nero B. viii. 47), requesting a loan. It is dated 1583, and states that they have already laid out "45,000 lbs.," and that this was not sufficient to defray their great charges. The text of the charter is preserved in Hakluyt, vol. ii.

He was an active trade organiser, and we find him the following year appointing Richard Elliott as Consul at Tripoli. In 1586 a charter was granted to fifty-three individuals to trade in the Levant, the principal mart being Aleppo, where Michael Lock had been established as Consul.

The leadership in the enterprise of which Master Fitch has left us so graphic an account, was entrusted to Master John Newberie—whose adventures will be described later on—to whom the Queen, as a mark of her cognisance and encouragement, granted the following letters missive to the Emperor Akbar and "the King of China":—

Elizabth to Akbar the Great Mogul.

"Elizabeth by the grace of God, &c. To the most inuincible, and most mightie prince, lord Zelabdim Echebar king of Cambaya. Inuincible Emperor, &c. The great affection which our Subiects haue to visit the most distant places of the world, not without good will and intention to introduce the trade of marchandize of al nations whatsoeuer they can, by which meanes the mutual and friendly trafique of marchandize on both sides may come, is the cause that the bearer of this letter Iohn Newbery, ioyntly with those that be in his company, with a curteous and honest boldnesse, doe repaire to the borders and countreys of your Empire, we doubt not but that your imperial Maiestie through your royal grace, will fauourably and friendly accept him. And that you would doe it the rather for our sake, to make vs greatly beholding to your Maiestie; wee should more earnestly, and with more wordes require it, if wee did think it needful. But by the singular report that is of your imperial Maiesties humanitie in these vttermost parts of the world, we are greatly eased of that burden, and therefore wee vse the fewer and lesse words : onely we request that because they are our subiects, they may be honestly intreated and receiued. And that in respect of the hard iourney which they haue vndertaken to places so far distant, it would please your Maiesty with some libertie and securitie of voiage to gratifie it, with such priuileges as to you shall seeme good : which curtesie if your Imperiall maiestie shal to our subiects at our requests performe, wee, according to our royall honour, wil recompence the same with as many deserts as we can. And herewith we bid your Imperial Maiestie to farewel."

To the "King of China."

"Elizabeth by the grace of God Queene of England, &c. Most Imperial and inuincible prince, our honest subiect Iohn Newbery the bringer hereof, who with our fauour hath taken in hand the voyage which nowe hee pursueth to the parts and countreys of your Empire, not trusting vpon any other ground then vpon the fauour of your Imperiall clemencie and humanitie, is mooued to vndertake a thing of so much difficultie, being perswaded that hee hauing entred into so many perils, your Maiestie will not dislike the same, especially, if it may appeare that it be not damageable vnto your royall Maiestie, and that to your people it will bring some profite: of both which things he not doubting, with more willing minde hath prepared himselfe for his destinated voyage vnto us well liked of. For by this meanes we perceiue, that the profit which by the mutual trade on both sides, al the princes our neighbors in ye West do receiue, your Imperial maiestie & those that be subiect vnder your dominion, to their great ioy and benefit shal haue the same, which consisteth in the transporting outward of such things whereof we haue plenty, & in bringing in such things as we stand in need of. It cannot otherwise be, but that seeing we are borne and made need one of another, & that wee are bound to aide one another, but that your imperial Maiestie wil wel like of it, & by your subiects w[t] like indeuor wil be accepted. For the increase whereof, if your imperial Maiestie shall adde the securitie of passage, with other priuileges most necessary to vse the trade with your men, your maiestie shall doe that which belongeth to a most honorable & liberal prince, and deserue so much of vs, as by no cōtinuance or length of time shal be forgotten. Which request of ours we do most instantly desire to be takē in good part of your maiestie, and so great a benefit towards vs & our men, we shall endeuor by diligence to requite when time shal serue thereunto. The God Almighty long preserue your Imperial maiestie." [1]

Sundry letters written during the journey will be given in their due order, but of all the party Fitch alone appears to have returned. In the introduction of his second volume, and in dedicating the book to Sir Robert Cecil, "principall Secretarie to her Maiestie," Hakluyt says that Fitch, "like another Paulus Venetus returned home to the place of his departure, with ample relation of his wonderful trauailes, which he presented in writing to my Lord your father, of honourable memorie," and further on he describes the traveller as "now liuing in London." [2]

[1] Both the letters are given in Hakluyt, vol. ii. part i.

[2] Sir Robert Cecil, son of the great Lord Burleigh, first came into prominence toward the end of 1592, when he was appointed one of the commissioners for the disposal of the contents of a valuable prize carrack which had been captured from the Spaniards and brought into Dartmouth. "He is the subject of an anecdote which Anthony Bacon, with a spice of malice, relates to the Earl of Essex. Lord Wemyss from Scotland, coming out from the Privy Chamber after an interview with the Queen,

The following is the story of the journey which was to lead to such pregnant results, given in the quaint English in which it was written three centuries ago, and with Hakluyt's marginal notes and comments. To some extent it must be admitted—as Mr. W. Foster, secretary of the Hakluyt Society, has suggested—that Fitch's relation is based on the framework of that of Cæsar Frederick, the Venetian merchant, which was Englished before his return in 1591. Cæsar Frederick left Venice twenty years earlier, in 1563, pursuing the same course to the Far East. There is certainly much similarity in the two accounts of the first portion of the common journey, from Tripoli to Aleppo and down the Euphrates and Tigris to Ormuz. But at this point our traveller begins an entirely new story, relates a new set of adventures, and even where the Venetian and the Englishman come to describe the same cities and scenes we have, in the following narrative, the advantage of looking at them for the first time through English eyes:—

NARRATIVE OF RALPH FITCH.[1]

"The voyage of M. Ralph Fitch marchant of London by the way of Tripolis in Syria, to Ormus,

asked the Lord Chamberlain for Sir Robert. 'Why, Sir,' said he, 'he was within.' 'By my soul,' saith the Lord Wemyss, 'I could not see him.' 'No marvel,' said Sir George Carey, 'being so little,' whereat the Lord Wemyss confessed he burst out of laughing" (Calendar of MS. preserved at Hatfield, parts iv. and v. Hist. MSS. Commission, 1892, 1894).

[1] From Hakluyt's "Principall Navigations," 1599–1600, vol. ii. part i.

and so to Goa in the East India, to Cambaia, and all the kingdome of Zelabdim Echebar the great Mogor, to the mighty riuer Ganges, and downe to Bengala, to Bacola, and Chonderi, to Pegu, to Iamahay in the kingdome of Siam, and backe to Pegu, and from thence to Malacca, Zeilan, Cochin, and all the coast of the East India: begunne in the yeere of our Lord 1583, and ended 1591, wherein the strange rites, maners, and customes of those people, and the exceeding rich trade and commodities of those countries are faithfully set downe and diligently described, by the aforesaid M. Ralph Fitch.

"In the yeere of our Lord 1583, I Ralph Fitch of London marchant being desirous to see the countreys of the East India, in the company of M. Iohn Newberie marchant (which had beene at Ormus once before) of William Leedes Ieweller, and Iames Story Painter, being chiefly set foorth by the right worshipfull Sir Edward Osborne knight, and M. Richard Staper citizens and marchants of London, did ship my selfe in a ship of London called the Tyger, wherein we went for Tripolis in Syria: & from thence we tooke the way for Aleppo, which we went in seuen dayes with the Carouan.[1] Being in Aleppo, and finding

[1] A member of the party who sailed in the *Tyger* was Master John Eldred, another London merchant and pioneer of note, of whom more anon. The following extract from Purchas (1625, book ix. chap. ix.) will be read with interest:—

good company, we went from thence to Birra, which is two dayes and an halfe trauaile with Camels.

Birra. "Birra is a little towne, but very plentifull of victuals: and neere to the wall of the towne runneth the riuer of Euphrates.[1] Here we bought a boate and agreed with a master and bargemen, for to go to Babylon. These boats be but for one voiage; for the streame doth runne so fast downewardes that they cannot returne. They carie you to a towne which they call Felugia, and there you sell the boate for a litle money, for that which cost you fiftie at Birra you sell there for seuen or eight. From Birra to Felugia is sixteene dayes iourney, it is not good that one boate

"Aleppo is called of the inhabitants Haleb, the chief Mart of all the East, frequented by Persians, Indians, Armenians and all Europeans. The Port is Scanderone, called by the Inhabitants Escanderuneh. The soyle is very fertile, & nourisheth abundance of Silke-wormes. . . . And besides other wealth innumerable, it hath eight Armories well furnished. It now flourisheth in the next place to Constantinople and Cairo, and may be called, Queen of the East: Here are store of Gems Ambar, Bengeoin, Lignum, Aloes & Muske." The Italian word Aleppo dates from the time when the Venetians dominated the Eastern trade, and it is stated that many Venetian families still survive and carry on characteristic industries. Commerce with Europe continues to pass chiefly through Scanderoon (Iskanderun), now better known as Alexandretta.

[1] Evidently Birejik or Bir, on the left bank of the Euphrates and at the head of the navigation on that river.

goe alone, for if it should chance to breake, you should haue much a doe to saue your goods from the Arabians, which be alwayes there abouts robbing: and in the night when your boates be made fast, it is necessarie that you keepe good watch. For the Arabians that bee theeues, will come swimming and steale your goods and flee away, against which a gunne is very good, for they doe feare it very much. In the riuer of Euphrates from Birra to Felugia there be certaine places where you pay custome, so many Medines [1] for a some or Camels lading, and certaine raysons and sope, which is for the sonnes of Aborise, which is Lord of the Arabians and all that great desert, and hath some villages vpon the riuer.

Felugia. Felugia where you vnlade your goods which come from Birra is a little village: from whence you goe to Babylon in a day.[2]

Babylon. "Babylon is a towne not very great but very populous, and of great traffike of strangers, for that is the way to Persia, Turkia and Arabia: and from thence doe goe Carouans for these and other places. Here are great store of victuals, which come from Armenia downe the

[1] A Turkish coin of small value.

[2] Feluja stands on the Euphrates W. by N. of Bagdad, with which city it is connected by the Sarsar Canal.

riuer of Tygris. They are brought vpon raftes made of goates skinnes blowne full of winde and bordes layde vpon them: and thereupon they lade their goods which are brought downe to Babylon, which being discharged they open their skinnes, and carry them backe by Camels, to serue another time. Babylon in times past did belong to the kingdome of Persia, but nowe is subiect to the Turke. Ouer against Babylon there is a very faire village from whence you passe to Babylon vpon a long bridge made of boats, and tyed to a great chaine of yron, which is made fast on either side of the riuer. When any boates are to passe vp or downe the riuer, they take away certaine of the boates vntill they be past.[1]

The Tower of Babel.

"The Tower of Babel is built on this side the riuer Tygris, towardes Arabia from the towne about seuen or eight

[1] Master Fitch refers to Bagdad. Purchas (book x. chap. vi.) testily observes in a marginal note, "Babilon (so vulgarly but falsely it is called), the true name is Bagdet;" he adds: "It is the Citie Royall of Mesopotamia, now called Diarbecr, which the said Almansur, placed in a large Plaine upon Tigris, and divided by the River into two Cities, joyned by a bridge of boats." Cæsar Frederick gives a similar account of "Babylon" on the Tigris, and a recent description of Bagdad states that a boat bridge still connects the two portions of the city. It is only when we come to the story of the "Tower of Babel" in Master Fitch's interesting narrative that some confusion arises.

miles, which tower is ruinated on all sides, and with the fall thereof hath made as it were a little mountaine, so that it hath no shape at all: it was made of brickes dried in the sonne, and certaine canes and leaues of the palme tree layed betwixt the brickes. There is no entrance to be seene to goe into it. It doth stand vpon a great plaine betwixt the riuers of Euphrates and Tygris.[1]

Boyling pitch continually issuing out of the earth.

"By the riuer Euphrates two dayes iourney from Babylon at a place called Ait, in a fielde neere vnto it, is a strange

[1] From this location, which accords with that of Cæsar Frederick, who, however, designates the remains "the Tower of Nimrod or Babel," Master Fitch may refer to the mound marking the great temple of Bel, the Babil or Mujellibe. A similar temple known as the Birs Nimroud, and generally believed by old travellers to be the veritable remains of the Tower of Babel, was built at the Babylonian suburb of Borsippa on the western side of Euphrates and is described by Layard in his "Discoveries in Nineveh and Babylon." It stands about six miles to the south-west of Hillah. Consisting of a great heap of bricks, slag, and broken pottery, "The dry nitrous earth of the parched plain, driven before the furious south wind, has thrown over the huge mass a thin covering of soil in which no herb or green thing can find nourishment or take root. Thus . . . the Birs Nimroud is ever a bare and yellow heap. It rises to the height of 198 feet, and has on its summit a compact mass of brickwork, 37 feet high by 28 broad (these dimensions are from Mr. Rich), the whole being thus 235 feet in perpendicular height." As Fitch was seized with sickness at Bagdad and afterwards continued his journey down the Tigris (see his letter from Goa), it is not likely that he crossed the Babylonian plain to view the Birs Nimroud.

thing to see: a mouth that doth continually throwe foorth against the ayre boyling pitch with a filthy smoke: which pitch doth runne abroad into a great fielde which is alwayes full thereof. The Moores say that it is the mouth of hell. By reason of the great quantitie of it, the men of that countrey doe pitch their boates two or three inches thicke on the outside, so that no water doth enter into them.[1] Their boates be called Danec. When there is great store of water in Tygris you may goe from Babylon to Basora in 8 or 9 dayes: if there be small store it will cost you the more dayes.

"Basora in times past was vnder the Arabians, but now is subiect to the Turke.[2] But some of them the Turke cannot subdue, for that they holde certaine Ilandes in the riuer Euphrates which the Turke cannot winne of them. They be theeues all and haue no setled dwelling, but remoue from place to place with their Camels, goates, and horses, wiues and children and all. They have large blew gownes, their wiues eares and noses are ringed very full of rings of copper and siluer, and

[1] The bituminous fountains of Hit (Chesney, vol. ii. p. 636).

[2] Busra, or Bussorah, is the principal Turkish port on the Persian Gulf.

they weare rings of copper about their legs.

"Basora standeth neere the gulfe of Persia, and is a towne of great trade of spices and drugges which come from Ormus. Also there is great store of wheate, ryce, and dates growing thereabout, wherewith they serue Babylon and all the countrey, Ormus, and all the partes of India. I went from Basora to Ormus downe the gulfe of Persia in a certaine shippe made of boordes, and sowed together with cayro, which is threede made of the huske of Cocoes, and certaine canes or strawe leaues sowed vpon the seames of the bordes which is the cause that they leake very much. And so hauing Persia alwayes on the left hande, and the coast of Arabia on the right hande we passed many Ilandes, and among others the famous Ilande Baharim from whence come the best pearles which be round and Orient.[1]

Ormus.

"Ormus is an Island in circuit about fiue and twentie or thirtie miles, and is the driest Island in the world: for there is nothing growing in it but onely salt: for their water, wood, or victuals, and all things necessary come out of Persia,

[1] Bahrein, or Aval Island: still noted for its pearl fisheries.

which is about twelue miles from thence.[1] All the Ilands thereabout be very fruitfull, from whence all kinds of victuals are sent vnto Ormus. The Portugales haue a castle here which standeth neere vnto the sea, wherein there is a Captaine for the king of Portugale hauing vnder him a conuenient number of souldiers, whereof some parte remaine in the castle, and some in the towne. In this towne are marchants of all Nations, and many Moores and Gentiles. Here is very great trade of all sortes of spices,

[1] The island of Ormuz, Hormuz, or Jerun, at the entrance to the Persian Gulf from the Gulf of Oman, is thirteen miles in circumference, and presents an extraordinary appearance from the sea, the mountains in the southern half being of variegated colours, from extensive impregnations of salt, sulphur, and other minerals. From the fourteenth to the seventeenth century it formed one of the richest trade depôts in the East. The great Albuquerque captured the place in 1507–8 in pursuit of his policy of destroying the commerce carried on by the Muhammadans with India. Professor Morse Stephens, in his "Albuquerque" (Rulers of India Series, Clarendon Press, 1892), states that the future viceroy, having taken part in the seizure of Socotra, intended to penetrate the Red Sea, but, having obtained a chart of the Persian Gulf made by a Muhammadan pilot, he went thither instead. "The wealth and prosperity of Ormuz is described in glowing terms by all early travellers in Asia, and it is called in ancient books 'the richest jewel set in the ring of the world.'" The British and Persians gained possession of the island in 1622, and Ormuz now belongs to Persia ; the trade, however, has been transferred to Bandar Abbas, the harbour has silted up, and there are but few inhabitants—fishermen and salt-diggers.

drugs, silke, cloth of silke, fine tapestrie of Persia, great store of pearles which come from the Isle of Baharim, and are the best pearles of all others, and many horses of Persia, which serue all India. They haue a Moore to their king which is chosen and gouerned by the Portugales. Their women are very strangely attyred, wearing on their noses, eares, neckes, armes and legges many rings set with iewels, and lockes of siluer and golde in their eares, and a long barre of golde vpon the side of their noses. Their eares with the weight of their iewels be worne so wide, that a man may thrust three of his fingers into them.

"Here very shortly after our arriuall wee were put in prison, and had part of our goods taken from vs by the Captaine of the castle, whose name was Don Mathias de Albuquerque; and from hence the eleuenth of October he shipped vs and sent vs for Goa vnto the Viceroy, which at that time was Don Francisco de Mascarenhas. The shippe wherein we were imbarked for Goa belonged to the Captaine, and carried one hundred twentie and foure horses in it. All marchandise carried to Goa in a shippe wherein are horses pay no custome in Goa. The horses pay custome, the goods pay nothing; but if you come in a ship which bringeth no horses, you are then to pay eight in the hundred for your goods.

Diu. "The first citie of India that we arriued at vpon the fift of Nouember, after we had passed the coast of Zindi,[1] is called Diu,[2] which standeth in an Iland in the kingdome of Cambaia, and is the strongest towne that the Portugales haue in those partes. It is but litle, but well stored with marchandise; for here they lade many great shippes with diuerse commodities for the streits of Mecca, for Ormus, and other places, and these be shippes of the Moores and of Christians. But the Moores cannot passe, except they haue a passeport from the Portugales. Cambaietta[3] is the chiefe citie of that prouince, which is great and very populous, and fairely builded for a towne of the Gentiles: but if there happen any famine, the people will sell their children for very little. The last king of Cambaia was Sultan Badu, which was killed at the siege of Diu, and shortly after his citie was taken by the great Mogor, which is the king of Agra and of Delli,

[1] Sind.

[2] The island of Diu is still in possession of the Portuguese.

[3] Cambay.

which are fortie dayes iourney from the country of Cambaia. Here the women weare vpon their armes infinite numbers of rings made of Elepsants teeth, wherein they take so much delight, that they had rather be without their meate then without their bracelets. Going from Diu we come to Damaan the second towne of the Portugales in the countrey of Cambaia which is distant from Diu fortie leagues.[1] Here is no trade but of corne and rice. They haue many villages vnder them which they quietly possesse in time of peace, but in time of warre the enemie is maister of them.

Daman.

"From thence we passed by Basaim, and from Basaim to Tana, at both which places is small trade but only of corne and rice. The tenth of Nouember we arriued at Chaul which standeth in the firme land. There be two townes, the one belonging to the Portugales, and the other to the Moores. That of the Portugales is neerest to the sea, and commaundeth the bay, and is walled round about. A little aboue that is the towne of the Moores which is gouerned

Basaim. Tana. Chaul.

[1] Daman in Guzerat also remains a Portuguese possession, and consists of a town and settlement covering an area of 82 square miles (Hunter's "Imperial Gazetteer of India").

by a Moore king called Xa-Maluco.[1] Here is great traffike for all sortes of spices and drugges, silke, and cloth of silke, sandales, Elephants teeth, and much China worke, and much sugar which is made of the nutte called Gagara: the tree is called the palmer: which is the profitablest tree in the worlde: it doth alwayes beare fruit, and doth yeeld wine, oyle, sugar, vineger, cordes, coles, of the leaues are made thatch for the houses, sayles for shippes, mats to sit or lie on: of the branches they make their houses, and broomes to sweepe, of the tree wood for shippes. The wine doeth issue out

[1] The travellers apparently passed into the Bassein inlet, separating the island of Salsette from the mainland where the chief town of the Tanna district, Bassein, now stands. It is recorded that the situation early attracted the notice of the Portuguese as affording a convenient rendezvous for shipping, and the town and land adjoining were ceded to them in 1534 by Shah Bahadur, King of Guzerat. The place grew to a position of considerable importance; it now forms portion of the Bombay Presidency (Hunter). John Huyghen van Linschoten (of whom more hereafter) in his "Voyage" (Hakluyt Society, 1885, vol. i.) thus describes this portion of the coast where the Portuguese had established forts: "first Daman from thence fifteene miles under 19 degrées and a halfe the town of Basaiin, from Basaiin ten miles under 19 degrées the Towne and fort of Chaul, from Chaul to Dabul are tenne miles, and lyeth under 18 degrées: from Dabul to the town and Island of Goa are 30 miles, which lyeth under 15 degrées and a halfe." It will be noticed that in the account of his return voyage Fitch gives the distance between Goa and Chaul as threescore leagues.

of the toppe of the tree. They cut a branch of a bowe and binde it hard, and hange an earthen pot vpon it, which they emptie euery morning and euery euening, and still it and put in certaine dried raysins, and it becommeth very strong wine in short time. Hither many shippes come from all partes of India, Ormus, and many from Mecca: heere be manie Moores and Gentiles. They haue a very strange order among them, they worshippe a cowe, and esteeme much of the cowes doung to paint the walles of their houses. They will kill nothing not so much as a louse: for they holde it a sinne to kille anything. They eate no flesh, but liue by rootes, and ryce, and milke. And when the husbande dieth his wife is burned with him, if shee be aliue: if she will not, her head is shauen, and then is neuer any account made of her after. They say if they should be buried, it were a great sinne, for of their bodies there would come many wormes and other vermine, and when their bodies were consumed, those wormes would lacke sustenance, which were a sinne, therefore they will be burned. In Cambaia they will kill nothing, nor haue anything killed: in the towne they haue hospitals to keepe lame dogs and cats, and for birds. They will giue meat to the Ants.

Goa. "Goa is the most principal citie which the Portugals haue in India, wherein the Viceroy remaineth with his court. It standeth in an Iland, which may be 25, or 30, miles about. It is a fine citie, and for an Indian towne very faire. The Iland is very faire, full of orchards and gardens, and many palmer trees, and hath some villages. Here bee many marchants of all nations. And the Fleete which commeth euery yeere from Portugal, which be foure, fiue, or sixe great shippes, commeth first hither. And they come for the most part in September, and remaine there fortie or fiftie dayes; and then goe to Cochin, where they lade their Pepper for Portugall. Oftentimes they lade one in Goa, the rest goe to Cochin which is from Goa an hundred leagues southward. Goa standeth in the countrey of Hidalcan, who lieth in the countrey sixe or seuen dayes iourney. His chiefe citie is called Bisapor.[1]

[1] "Hidalcan" is probably a corruption of the title of the ruler of the Mussulman state of Bijapur, the Adil Shah, or Khan. Ibrahim Adil II., then an infant, succeeded his uncle Ali Adil Shah in 1579, and on assuming the government ruled with ability, dying in 1626 (Hunter).

This was the 20[1] of Nouember.

"At our comming we were cast into the prison, and examined before the Iustice, and demanded for letters, and were charged to be spies, but they could prooue nothing by vs. We continued in prison vntill the two and twentie of December, and then we were set at libertie, putting in sureties for two thousand duckats not to depart the towne; which sureties father Steuens an English Iesuite which we found there, & another religious mā a friend of his procured for vs. Our sureties name was Andreas Taborer, to whom we paid 2150. duckats, and still he demaunded more: where vpon we made sute to the Viceroy and Iustice to haue our money againe, considering that they had had it in their hands neere fiue moneths and could prooue nothing against vs. The Viceroy made vs a very sharpe answere, and sayde wee should be better sifted before it were long, and that they had further matter against vs. Wherevpon we presently determined rather to seeke our liberties, then to bee in danger for euer to be slaues in the country, for it was told vs we should haue ye strapado. Wherevpon presently, the fift day of April 1585. in the morning we ranne from

[1] Fitch himself gives the date November 29, see page 65.

> thence. And being set ouer the riuer, we went two dayes on foote not without feare, not knowing the way nor hauing any guide, for we durst trust none."

[Some curious details of the imprisonment and escape of the adventurers will be found in the following chapter. The narrative is continued on page 92.]

CHAPTER II

DETAILS OF THE ARREST AND ESCAPE—A FRIEND IN NEED—NEWBERIE'S LAST LETTER—"GOLDEN GOA"—PORTUGUESE IN INDIA

FURTHER particulars of the experiences of the four travellers at Goa are given in the correspondence they sent home and happily preserved in Hakluyt's Collection (vol. ii.). But even more interest attaches to the independent account of their arrival, detention, and escape given by John Huyghen van Linschoten, the Netherlander, who, as a pioneer of discovery and commerce, stands to his own countrymen at least in quite as prominent a position as Fitch occupies in regard to the East India Company. This was the most critical episode in the voyage, and it may be suggested that Fitch's and Newberie's letters reproduced in this chapter were written with due caution.

Ralph Fitch to Leonard Poore.

The following is the text of a letter written, during his arrest, by Master Ralph Fitch to his friend Master Leonard Poore of London:—

SCENE IN THE MARKET PLACE AT GOA.

"Louing friend Master Poore, &c. Since my departure from Aleppo, I haue not written vnto you any letters, by reason that at Babylon, I was sicke of the fluxe, and being sicke, I went from thence for Balsara, which was twelue dayes iourney downe the riuer Tygris, where we had extreme hot weather, which was good for my disease, ill fare, and worse lodging, by reason our boat was pestered with people. In eight daies, that which I did eate was very small, so that if we had stayed two dayes longer vpon the water, I thinke I had died: but comming to Balsara, presently I mended, I thanke God. There we stayed 14 dayes, and then we imbarked our selues for Ormuz, where we arriued the fifth of September, and were put in prison the ninth of the same moneth, where we continued vntill the 11 of October, and then were shipt for this citie of Goa in the captaines ship, with an 114 horses, and about 200 men: and passing by Diu & Chaul, where we went on land to water the 20 of Nouember, we arriued at Goa the 29 of the said moneth, where for our better intertainment we were presently put into a faire strong prison, were we continued vntil the 22 of December. It was the will of God that we found there 2 Padres, the one an Englishman, the other a Flemming. The Englishmans name is Padre Thomas Steuens, the others Padre Marco, of the order of S. Paul. These did sue for vs vnto the Viceroy and other officers, and stood vs in as much stead, as our liues and goods were woorth: for if they had not stucke to vs, if we had escaped with our liues, yet we had had long imprisonment.

"After 14 dayes imprisonment they offered vs, if we could put in suerties for 2000 duckats, we should goe abroad in the towne: which when we could not doe, the said Padres found suerties for vs, that we should not depart the countrey without the licence of the Viceroy. It doth spite the Italians to see vs abroad: and many maruell at our deliuery. The painter is in the cloister of S. Paul, and is of their order, and liketh there very well. While we were in prison both at Ormuz and here, there was a great deale of our goods pilfered and lost, and we haue beene at great charges in gifts and otherwise, so that a great deale of our goods is consumed. There is much of our things which wil sell very well, & some we shall get nothing for. I hope in God that at the returne of the Viceroy, which is gone to Chaul and to Diu, they say, to winne a castle of the Moores, whose returne is thought will be about Easter, then we shall get our libertie, and our suerties discharged. Then I thinke it wil be our best way, either one or both to returne, because our troubles haue bene so great, & so much of our goods spoyled and lost. But if it please God that I come into England, by Gods helpe, I will returne hither againe. It is a braue and pleasant countrey, and very fruitfull. The summer is almost all the yeere long, but the chiefest at Christmas.

"The day and the night are all of one length, very little difference, and marueilous great store of fruits. For all our great troubles yet are we fat and well liking, for victuals are here plentie and good cheape. And here I will passe ouer to certifie you of strange things, vntil our meeting, for it would be too long to write thereof. And thus I commit you to God, who euer preserue you and vs all. From Goa in the East Indies the 25 of Januarie 1584. Yours to command, Ralph Fitch."

Linschoten's story.

The following account of the arrival and secret departure of the Englishmen is given by John Huyghen van Linschoten, the young Dutchman who was in the train of the Archbishop of Goa. He may be accepted as an entirely unbiassed witness. His animadversions concerning the Jesuits and their designs contrast strangely with the terms of respect, not to say affection, in which he refers here and elsewhere to his master, the archbishop, who exerted a beneficent influence on behalf of the English prisoners. The reprint is from "The Voyage of John Huyghen van Linschoten to the East Indies, from the old English translation of 1598, the first book containing his description of the East," in two volumes, published by the Hakluyt Society. The first volume was edited by the late Dr. A. C. Burnell, and the second by Mr. P. A. Tiele, of Utrecht. Dr. Burnell expresses the opinion that the original English version was poorly done, and he has adopted the method of bracketing the redundancies in the text and giving important corrections in footnotes, a plan followed by Mr. Tiele. The late Sir Henry Yule and Dr. Kern have also added explanatory notes. In the following extract most of the disputed passages are ignored and only the most important footnotes are reproduced. A brief biographical sketch of Linschoten, with some account of the great service he rendered in the opening up of the East, will be found in a latter portion of this work (page 213):—

"In the moneth of December,[1] Anno, 1583, there arived in the towne and Island of Ormus foure Englishmen, which came from Aleppo in the countrie of Suria, having sayled out of England, and passed through the straightes of Gibraltar, to Tripoli a towne and Haven, lying on the sea coast of Suria, where all the shippes discharge their marchandises, and from thence are caryed by land unto Aleppo,

[1] September. See Newberie and Fitch's letters.

which is nyne dayes iourney. In Aleppo there are resident marchants of all Nations, as Italians, Frenchemen, Englishmen, Armenians, Turkes, & Mores, everie man having his Religion apart, paying tribute unto the great Turke. In that towne there is great trafficke, for that from thence, everie yeare there travelleth two Caffylen,[1] that is, companies of people and Camelles, which travell unto India, Persia, Arabia, and all the countries bordering on the same, and deale in all sorts of marchandise, both to and from those Countries, as I in an other place have alreadie declared. Three of the said Englishmen aforesaide were sent by the Companie of Englishmen, in Aleppo, to see if in Ormus they might keepe any Factors, and so trafficke in that place, like as also the Italians doe, that is to say, the Venetians, which in Ormus, Goa and Malacca have their Factors, and trafficke there, as well for stones and pearles, as for other wares and spices of those countries, which are caryed over land into Venice. One of these Englishmen had beene once before in Ormus, and there had taken good information of the trade, and upon his advise the other were come thether, bringing great store of marchandises with them, as Clothes, Saffron, all kindes of glasses, knives, and such like stuffe, to conclude, all kinde of small wares that may be devised. And although those wares amounted unto great summes of money, notwithstanding it was but onlie a shadow or colour, thereby to give no occasion to be mistrusted: for that their principall intent was to buy great quantities of precious Stones, as Diamantes, Pearles, Rubies, &c., to the which ende they brought with them a great summe of money and Gold, and that verie secretly [not to be decyved or robbed thereof], or to runne into anie danger for the same. They being thus in Ormus, hyred a Shop, and began to sell their wares: which the Italians perceyving, whose Factors con-

[1] Caravans.

tinue there (as I sayd before) and fearing that those Englishmen, finding good vent for their commodities in that place wold be resident therein, and so daylie increase, which would be no small losse and hinderance unto them, did presently invent all the subtile meanes they could, to hinder them: and to that end they went unto the Captaine of Ormus, as then called Don Gonsalo de Meneses, telling him that there were certaine Englishmen come unto Ormus, that were sent only to spy the Country, and said further, that they were Heretickes: and therefore they sayd it was convenient they should not be suffered to depart, without beeing examined, and punished to the example of others.

"The Captaine being a friend unto the Englishmen, by reason that one of them which had bene there before, had given him certaine presents, would not be perswaded to trouble them, but shipped them with all their wares in a Shippe that was to sayle for Goa, and sent them to the Viceroy, that he might examine and trye them, as hee thought good: where when they were aryved, they were cast into prison, and first examined whether they were good Christians: and because they could speake but bad Portugale, onlie two of them spake good Dutche, as having bene certaine yeares in the lowe Countries, and there traffiqued, there was a Dutch Iesuite borne in the towne of Brigges in Flaunders,[1] that had bin resident in the Indies for the space of thirty yeares, sent unto them, to examine them: wherein they had behaved themselves so wel, that they were holden for good and Catholick Romish Christians: yet still suspected, because they were strangers, specially Englishmen. The Iesuites stil told them that they shuld be sent prisoners into Portingal, wishing them to become Iesuites, promising them thereby to defend them from all

[1] Bruges. Fitch, it will be observed, calls this man "Padre Marco," and Newberie "Padre Marke." It is curious to compare their statements regarding him with that of Linschoten.

trouble: the cause why they perswaded them in that earnest manner was, for that the Dutch Iesuite had secretlie bene advertised of great summes of money which they had about them, and sought to get the same into their fingers, for that the first vowe and promise (of) their order, is, to procure the welfare of their said order, by what means soever it be, but although the Englishmen denyed them, and refused the order, saying, that they were unfit for such places, neverthelesse they proceed so farre that one of them, being a painter, (that came with the other three for company to see the countries, and to seeke his fortune, and was not sent thether by the English marchants) partly for feare, and partlie for want of meanes, promised them to become a Iesuite: and although they knew he was not any of those that had the treasure, yet because he was a Painter, whereof they are but few in India, and that they had great need of him to paint their church, which otherwise would cost them great charges, to bring one from Portingal, they were glad, hoping in time to get the rest of them with all their money: so yt. to conclude, they made this Painter a Iesuite, where he continued certain daies giving him good store of worke to doe, and entertayning him with all the favour and friendship they could devise, and all to win the rest, to be a pray for them; but the other three continued still in prison, being in great feare, because they understood no man that came to them, nor anie man almost knew what they said: till in the end it was told them that certaine Dutch men dwelt in the Archbishops house, & counsell given them to send unto them, whereat they much reioiced, and sent to me and an other Dutch man,[1] desiring us once to come and speake with them, which we presentlie did, and they with teares in their eyes made complaint unto us of their hard usage, from point to point (as it is said before) desiring us, if we might

[1] Bernard Burcherts, of Hamburg, who was a member of the archbishop's suite. Linschoten says he returned home in 1585.

to helpe them, that they might be set at liberty upon Sureties, being readie to indure what Iustice should ordaine for them, saying that if it were found contrarie, and that they were other then travelling marchants, and sought to find out [further] benefite by their wares, they would be content to be punished.

"With that wee departed from them promising them to do our best: and in the ende we obtained so much of the Archbishoppe, that he went unto the Vice-roy to delyver our petition, and perswaded him so well, that hee was content to set them at libertie and that their goods shuld be delivered unto them again, upon condition they should put in sureties for 2000. Pardawes, not to depart the countrie before other order should bee taken with them. Therupon they presently found a Citizen of the towne, yt. was their suretie for 2000. Pardawes, where they paide him in hand 1300. Pardawes, and because they say they had no more ready monie, he gave them credite, seeing what store of marchandise they had, whereby at all times if neede were, hee might bee satisfied: and by that meanes they were delivered out of prison, and hyred a house, and began to set open shoppe: So that they uttered much ware, and were presently well knowne because they alwaies respected Gentlemen, specially such as brought [1] their wares, shewing great curtesie and honor unto them, whereby they wonne much credite, and were beloved of all men, so that everie man favoured them, and was willing to doe them pleasure. To us they shewed great friendship, for whose sake, the Archbishop favoured them much, and shewed them verie good countenance, which they knew wel how to increase, by offering him many presents, although hee would not receive them, neither would ever take gift or present at any mans hands. Likewise they behaved themselves verie Catholikely and devoute, everie day hearing Masse with

[1] Bought.

Beades in their hands, so that they fel into so great favour, that no man caried an evill eye, no nor an evill thought towards them. Which liked not the Iesuites, because it hindered them from that they hoped for, so that they ceased not still by this Dutch Iesuite to put them in feare, that they should bee sent into Portingall to the King, counselling them to yeeld them selves into their Cloyster, which if they did, he said they would defend them from all saying further, that he counselled them therein as friend, and one that knew for certaine that it was determined by the Viceroyes privie Counsell: which to effect he saide they stayed but for shipping that should sayle for Portingall, with divers other perswasions, to put them in some feare, & so to effect their purpose.

"The English men durst not say any thing to them, but answered, that as yet they would stay a while, and consider thereof, thereby putting the Iesuites in good comfort, as one among them, being the principal of them (called John Nuberye) complained unto me often times, saying hee knew not which way he might be rid of those troubles: but in the ende they determined with themselves, to depart from thence, and secretly by means of contrarie friends, they imployed their money in precious stones, which the better to effect, one of them was a Ieweller,[1] and for the same purpose came with them. Which being concluded among them, they durst not make knowne to any man, neither did they credite us so much, although they tolde us all whatsoever they knew. But on a Whitsunday they went abroad to sport themselves about three miles from Goa, in the mouth of the ryver in a countrie called Bardes, having with them good store of meate and drinke. And because they should not be suspected, they left their house and shop,

[1] Mr. Tiele gives the original Dutch, *Steen-slyper* (polisher of precious stones).

with some wares therein unsolde, in custodie of a Dutch Boy, by us provided for them, that looked unto it. This Boye was in the house not knowing their intent, and being in Bardes, they had with them a Patamar,[1] which is one of the Indian postes, which in winter times caryeth letters from one place to the other, whom they had hyred to guide them: & because that betweene Bardes and the Firm land there is but a little ryver, halfe drie, they passed over it on foote, and so travelled by land, being never heard of againe: but it is thought they arrived in Aleppo, as some say, but they knew not certainely. Their greatest hope was, that John Newbery could speake the Arabian tongue, which is used in al those countries, or at the least understoode, for it is very common in all places there abouts, as French with us.

"Newes being come to Goa, there was a great stirre and murmuring among the people, and we much wondered at it: for many were of opinion, that wee had given them counsel so to doe, and presently their suertie seased upon the goods remaining, which might amount unto above 200. Pardawes, and with that and the money he had received of the English men, he went unto the Viceroye, and delivered it unto him, which the Viceroy having received, forgave him the rest. This flight of the English men grieved the Iesuites most, because they had lost such a pray, which they made sure account of, whereupon the Dutch Iesuite came to us to aske us if we knew thereof, saying, that if he had suspected so much, he would have dealt otherwise, for that he said, hee once had in his hands of theirs a bagge wherein was fortie thousand Veneseanders (each Veneseander being two Pardawes) which was when they were in

[1] "*Patamar*, or *Pattimar*, in modern usage is a kind of vessel on the west coast. But in all the writers of the sixteenth and seventeenth centuries it is a foot-runner or courier, from Konkani, *pathmar*, a courier" (Yule).

prison.[1] And that they had alwayes put him in comfort, to accomplish his desire, upon the which promise hee gave them their money againe, which otherwise they shoulde not so lightly have come by, or peradventure never, as hee openly said : and in the ende he called them hereticks, and spies, with a thousand other rayling speeches, which he uttered against them.

"The Englishman that was become a Iesuite, hearing that his companions were gone, and perceiving that the Iesuites shewed him not so great favour, as they did at the first, repented himselfe, and seeing he had not as then made any solemne promise, & being counselled to leave the house [& told] that he could not want a living in the towne, as also that the Iesuites could not keepe him there without he were willing to stay, for they could not accuse him of any

[1] Original Dutch, "Venetseanders," *i.e.*, ducats of Venice (Tiele). "The partab (pratap) was a gold coin found current in India, and adopted by the Portuguese ; but the latter coined silver pardáos of much smaller value, and the determination of a pardáo at different periods is difficult. If the Venetseander was a zecchin, those here in question must have been gold pardáos, which were worth half a gold pagoda" (Yule).

Linschoten (vol. i.) devotes a chapter to "money, weight, and measure of India, and Goa." In an editorial footnote Dr. Burnell calls attention to the fact that in Hakluyt's translation of Cæsar Frederick a pagoda is said to be a gold coin, worth 6s. 8d. sterling (at Goa) ; while the original Italian puts a pagoda at eight lira "of our money" (*i.e.*, Venetian). By the above calculation a venetseander was equal in value to a gold pagoda, which was worth 6s. 8d. sterling at that time. Therefore the worthy Dutch Jesuit told his countrymen, in effect, that the English travellers, notwithstanding their untoward experiences, were still in possession of a "bagge" containing cash equivalent in those days to over £13,000, or about £78,000 in these times ! John Eldred, a fellow traveller for part of the journey, tells a very different story (see p. 218).

thing: he told them flatly, that he had no desire to stay within the Cloyster, and although they used all the meanes they could to keepe him there, yet hee would not stay, but hyred a house without the Cloyster, and opened shop, where he had good store of worke, and in the end married a Mesticos daughter of the towne, so that hee made his account, to stay there while he lived. By this Englishman I was instructed of al the waies, trades, and viages of the countrie, betweene Aleppo and Ormus, and of all the ordinances and common customes, which they usually hold during their Viage over land, as also of the places and townes wher they passed. And since those Englishmens departures from Goa, there never arrived any strangers either English or others by land in the sayde countries, but onely Italyans which daylye traffique over land, and use continuall trade going and comming that way."

Master John Newberie's story.

The appended letters are given here because they deal chiefly with the arrest and imprisonment. The first two from Ormuz are addressed to John Eldred and William Shals (or Shales) at Bassorah:—

"Right welbeloued and my assured good friends, I heartily cōmend me vnto you, hoping of your good healths, &c. To certifie you of my voiage, after I departed frō you, time wil not permit: but the 4 of this present we arriued here, & the 10 day I with the rest were committed to prison, and about the middle of the next moneth, the Captaine wil send vs all in his ship for Goa. The cause why we are taken, as they say, is, for that I brought letters from Don Antonio.[1] But the trueth is, Michael Stropene,

[1] The Portuguese Pretender, and in some sort the *protégé* of England.

was the onely cause, vpon letters that his brother wrote him from Aleppo. God knoweth how we shall be delt withall in Goa, and therefore if you can procure our masters to send the king of Spaine his letters for our releasement, you should doe vs great good: for they cannot with iustice put vs to death. It may be that they will cut our throtes, or keepe vs long in prison: Gods will be done. All those commodities that I brought hither, had beene very well sold, if this trouble had not chanced. You shall do well to send with all speed a messenger by land from Balsara to Aleppo, for to certifie of this mischance, although it cost thirtie or forty crownes, for that we may be the sooner released, and I shalbe the better able to recouer this againe which is now like to be lost: I pray you make my hearty commendations, &c. From out of the prison in Ormuz, this 21 of September, 1583."

"The barke of the Iewes is arriued here two daies past, by whom I know you did write, but your letters are not like to come to my handes. This bringer hath shewed me here very great courtesie, wherefore I pray you shew him what fauor you may. About the middle of the next moneth I thinke we shall depart from hence, God be our guide. I thinke Andrew will goe by land to Aleppo, wherein I pray you further him what you may: but if he should not goe, then I pray you dispatch away a messenger with as much speede as possible you may. I can say no more, but do for me as you would I should do for you in the like cause, and so with my very hearty commendations, &c. From out of the prison in Ormuz, this 24 day of September, 1583."

His letter to Leonard Poore

The next letter, dated a few days earlier than that of Master Fitch's (see pp. 65–6), but doubtless despatched at the same time, is possessed of pathetic interest from the fact that it appears to be the last communication from this enterprising traveller received in this country:—

"My last I sent you was from Ormuz, whereby I certified you what had happened there vnto me, and the rest of my company, which was, that foure dayes after our arriuall there, we were all committed to prison, except one Italian which came with me from Aleppo, whom the Captaine neuer examined, onely demaunded what countryman he was, but I make account Michael Stropene, who accused vs, had informed the Captaine of him. The first day we arriued there, this Stropene accused vs that we were spies sent from Don Antonio, besides diuers other lies; notwithstanding if we had beene of any other countrey then of England, we might freely haue traded with them.[1] And although we be Englishmen, I know no reason to the contrary, but that we may trade hither and thither as well as other nations, for all nations doe, and may come freely to Ormuz, as Frenchmen, Flemmings, Almains, Hungarians, Italians, Greekes, Armenians, Nazaranies, Turkes and Moores, Iewes & Gentiles, Persians, Moscouites, and there is no nation that they seeke for to trouble, except ours: wherefore it were contrary to all iustice and reason that they should suffer all nations to trade with them, and to forbid vs. But now I haue as great libertie as any other nation, except it be to go out of the countrey, which thing as yet I desire not. But I thinke hereafter, and before it be long, if I shall be desirous to go from hence, that they wil not deny me licence. Before we might be suffered to come out of prison, I was forced to put in suerties for 2000 pardaus, not to depart from hence without licence of the viceroy: otherwise except this, we haue as much libertie as

[1] A suggestive passage which shows that Newberie, at least, realised the political dangers of the journey.

any other nation, for I haue our goods againe, & haue taken an house in the chiefest streete in the towne, called the Rue drette, where we sell our goods.

"There were two causes which moued the captaine of Ormus to imprison vs, & afterwards to send vs hither. The first was, because Michael Stropene had accused vs of many matters, which were most false. And the second was for that M. Drake at his being at Maluco, caused two pieces of his ordinance to be shot at a gallion of the kings of Portugall, as they say. But of these things I did not know at Ormus: and in the ship that we were sent in came the chiefest iustice in Ormus, who was called Aueador generall of that place, he had beene there three yeeres, so that now his time was expired: which Aueador is a great friend of the captaine of Ormus, who, certain days after our comming from thence, sent for mee into his chamber, and there beganne to demaund of me many things, to the which I answered: and amongst the rest, he said, that Master Drake was sent out of England with many ships, and came to Maluco, and there laded cloues, and finding a gallion there of the kings of Portugall, hee caused two pieces of his greatest ordinance to be shot at the same: and so perceiuing that this did greatly grieue them, I asked, if they would be reuenged of me for that which M. Drake had done: To the which he answered, No: although his meaning was to the contrary.

"He said moreouer, that the cause why the captaine of Ormus did send me for Goa, was, for that the Viceroy would vnderstand of mee, what newes there was of Don Antonio, and whether he were in England, yea or no, and that it might be all for the best that I was sent hither, the which I trust in God wil so fall out, although contrary to his expectation: for had it not pleased God to put into the minds of the archbishop and other two Padres or Iesuits of S. Pauls colledge to stand our friends, we might haue rotted in prison. The archbishop is a very good man, who hath two yong men to his seruantes, the one of them was borne at Hamborough, and is called Bernard Borgers: and the other was borne at Enchuysen, whose name is Iohn Linscot, who did vs great pleasure: for by them the archbishop was many times put in minde of vs.[1] And the two good fathers of S. Paul, who trauelled very much for us, the one of them is called Padre Marke, who was borne in Bruges in Flanders, and the other was borne in Wilshire in England, and is called Padre Thomas Steuens.

"Also I chanced to finde here a young man, who was borne in Antwerpe, but the most part of his bringing vp hath beene in London, his name is Francis de Rea, and with him it was my hap to be acquainted in Aleppo, who also hath done me great pleasure here.

"In the prison at Ormus we remained many dayes, also we lay a long time at sea comming hither, and forthwithe at our arriuall here were carried to prison, and the next day after were sent for before the Aueador, who is the chiefest iustice, to be examined: and when we were examined, he presently sent vs backe againe to prison.

"And after our being here in prison 13 daies, Iames Storie went into the monastery of S. Paul, where he remaineth, and is made one of the company, which life he liketh very well.

"And vpon S. Thomas day (which was 22 dayes after our arriuall here) I came out of prison, and the next day after came out Ralph Fitch and William Bets.[2]

"If these troubles had not chanced, I had beene in possibility to haue made as good a voyage as euer any man made with so much money. Many of our things I haue solde very well, both here and at Ormus in prison, notwithstanding the captaine willed me (if I would) to sell what

[1] Burcherts and Linschoten.

[2] No doubt William Leedes is referred to.

I could before we imbarked: & so with officers I went diuers times out of the castle in the morning, and solde things, and at night returned againe to the prison, and all things that I solde they did write, and at our imbarking from thence, the captain gaue order that I should deliuer all my mony with the goods into the hands of the scriuano, or purser of the ship, which I did, and the scriuano made a remembrance, which he left there with the captaine, that myselfe and the rest with money & goods he should deliuer into the hands of the Aueador generall of India: but at our arriuall here, the Aueador would neither meddle with goods nor money, for that he could not proue anything against vs: wherefore the goods remained in the ship 9 or 10 daies after our arriuall, and then, for that the ship was to saile from thence, the scriuano sent the goods on shore, and here they remained a day and a night, and no body to receiue them. In the end they suffered this bringer to receiue them, who came with me from Ormus, and put them into an house which he had hired for me, where they remained foure or fiue daies. But afterward when they should deliuer the money, it was concluded by the iustice, that both the money and goods should be deliuered into the positors hands, where they remained fourteene dayes after my comming out of prison. At my being in Aleppo, I bought a fountaine of siluer and gilt, sixe kniues, sixe spoones, and one forke trimmed with corall for fiue and twentie chekins, which the captaine of Ormus did take, and payed for the same twentie pardaos, which is one hundred larines, and was worth there or here one hundred chekins. Also he had fiue emrauds set in golde, which were woorth fiue hundred or sixe hundred crownes, and payed for the same an hundred pardaos. Also he had nineteene and a halfe pikes of cloth, which cost in London twentie shillings the pike, and was worth 9 or 10 crownes the pike, and he payed for the same twelue larines a pike. Also he had two

PORTUGUESE GENTLEMEN AT GOA.

pieces of greene Kersies, which were worth foure and twentie pardaos the piece, and payd for them sixteene pardaos a piece: besides diuers other trifles, that the officers and others had in the like order, and some for nothing at all. But the cause of all this was Michael Stropene, which came to Ormus not woorth a penie, and now hath thirtie or fortie thousand crownes, and he grieueth that any other stranger should trade thither but himselfe. But that shall not skill, for I trust in God to goe both thither and hither, and to buy and sell as freely as he or any other. Here is very great good to be done in diuers of our commodities, and in like manner there is great profite to be made with commodities of this countrey, to be carried to Aleppo.

"It were long for me to write, and tedious for you to read of all things that haue passed since my parting from you. But of all the troubles that haue chanced since mine arriuall in Ormus, this bringer is able to certifie you. I mind to stay here: wherefore if you will write vnto me, you may send your letters to some friend at Lisbone, & frō thence by the ships they may be conueyed hither. Let the direction of your letters be either in Portuguise or Spanish, whereby they may come the better to my hands. From Goa this 20 day of Januarie, 1584."

Goa in the sixteenth century.

We have already seen what were Master Fitch's impressions of "Golden Goa," that gate to the opulent and mysterious East the fame of which had already spread over Europe; possibly the nature of his reception somewhat damped the ardour of his description. Cæsar Frederick, who visited Goa in 1567, and again in 1570 when it was besieged by the King of Bijapur, states that there was great traffic but that the island was fairer than the city, being full of goodly gardens. In Linschoten's interesting work, however, we find probably the most complete picture of this great emporium in the heyday of its prosperity. Goa he describes as well built, with houses and streets interspersed with gardens and orchards, but of the widespread immorality of the place he tells us more than enough. He gives an amusing account of the punctiliousness of the Portuguese residents, many of whom lived in considerable "style." On the other hand the soldiery, a term which appears to have included all the single men of little or no means or without civil employment, fared very poorly, except on occasions when volunteers were called up for an expedition. The daily life of Goa was stimulated by a morning market, or fair, to which all classes and kindreds flocked, except on holy days, which were observed with considerable pomp. He adds a statement which is of no little importance coming as it does from a member of the Archbishop's household, to the effect that the laws observed were those of Portugal and that the people of all nations dwelling there—Indians, Moors, Jews, Armenians, &c.—were allowed to practise their own religions, the only prohibitions being in regard to suttee and similar rites. The fact that one of the charges upon which the Englishmen had been detained was that they were "Heretickes," does not detract from the value of his general assertion of religious freedom. Protestantism, in the eyes of all Spanish subjects at least, means something more than a difference in religious faith.

Portuguese rule.

A very brief sketch of the rise and development of Portuguese power in the East up to this time will not be out of place here, some notes on their operations in the Further East being reserved for a later chapter. Bartholomew Dias, sailing at the command of John II. of Portugal, 1486, was the first navigator to double the Cape of Good Hope, reaching Algoa Bay. He was followed by Vasco de Gama who, anchoring his three ships off Calicut, 1498, proved to be the pioneer of Portuguese power in India. The new arrivals first opened negotiations with the Zamorin of Calicut, the suzerain of the various kings or rajas on the Malabar coast, but in the beginning discovered that they had formidable rivals in the Muhammadan Arabs, or Moors as they called them. These traders had long enjoyed the Indian monopoly, sending their goods either to the Persian Gulf or, *viâ* Suez and Alexandria, to the Mediterranean. But by common consent the great Albuquerque, governor and captain-general, 1509–15, was the real founder of the Portuguese dominion in the East. Whatever may now be thought of his methods, his hectoring and his savagery, he followed a consistent policy. He broke down the Moorish monopoly, and actually threatened the Turkish Sultan in his own dominions.[1] Establishing his

[1] Prof. Stephens (*q.v.*) repeats the extraordinary story that among the plans contemplated by Albuquerque for the destruction of Muhammadan rivalry was one for the diversion of the course of the Nile, through Abyssinia to the Red Sea, in order to ruin Egypt; while another was to seize the body of Muhammad.

capital in the island of Goa, which long flourished as a monument to his genius, his personal conquests extended from Ormuz to Malacca. At the time of his death, which took place on the bar of Goa in 1515, peace, so called, was universal from Ormuz to Ceylon; and from Cape Comorin eastward the King of Portugal was on terms of friendship with the kings of Pegu, Bengal, Pedir, Siam, Pacem, Java and China, the King of Maluco and the Gores.[1] Without attempting even a chronological summary of events in India between the year of Albuquerque's death and the period under notice, it is interesting to quote what may be described as the official view, and thus to trace the commencement of decay. Faria y Sousa, the well-known Portuguese poet and historian (1590–1649), who was sometime secretary to the Marquis of Castel Rodrigo, ambassador at Rome, thus signalises the preferment of Lopo Soarez de Albegaria, the next governor: "Till this time the Gentlemen had followed the Dictates of true Honor, esteeming their Arms the greatest Riches; from this time forwards they so wholly gave up themselves to trading, that those who had been Captains became Merchants, so that what had been Command became a Shame, Honor was a Scandal, and Reputation a Reproach." During the same Viceroyalty

[1] Mr. F. C. Danvers in his "Portuguese in India" (W. H. Allen & Co., 1894), quoted above, gives an interesting account of the last days of Albuquerque and of his work. He summarises the results of his labours in India from the Viceroy's famous "Commentaries," which have been edited for the Hakluyt Society by Mr. Walter de Gray Birch.

(1517) the chronicler records the arrival of Alcacova (or Alcaceva) as surveyor of the royal revenues, and his return in disgust to Portugal. He adds, "Hence began the hearing Complaints against the Governors and Commanders of India, and hence it was that many took more care to heap Riches than Honor, knowing them to be a protection against all Crimes."[1] Linschoten himself at a later date speaks pretty plainly on the evils of the government of the Viceroys: "There is not one of them," he says, "that esteemeth the profit of the commonwealth, or the furtherance of the king's service, but rather their own particular commodities," and he adds that the same rotten system existed in all the stations in India.

Still, although the principal figure had departed, the great work of Portuguese exploitation went on. "Dom Francisco Mascarenhas, Count of Santa Cruz," who received our travellers in the manner described in this volume, "was the first Viceroy sent to India after the subjugation of the kingdom of Portugal by the King of Spain. He had already had considerable experience in India, where he had greatly distinguished himself by the gallant defence of the city of Chaul with a few men, and no wall, against the power of Nizamaluco, who had besieged it with 150,000 men.[2] Dom Francisco was accom-

[1] "Portuguese Asia," Stevens's translation, 1695, vol. ii., pp. 210, 216.

[2] Nizamaluco appears to have been derived by the earlier voyagers from the name Nizam-al-Mulk (see note to Linschoten, vol. i. p. 168).

panied by a fleet of five ships, and on arrival at Goa on the 16th of September, 1581, he found all India had already proclaimed King Philip, in accordance with the instructions that had previously been sent to the Governor, Fernão Telles de Menezes."[1] He was succeeded by Dom Duarte de Menezes, who left Lisbon in the spring of 1584. During this vice-royalty, which extended to 1588, when Menezes died, important changes were attempted in the methods of Indian trade. In order to raise funds to prosecute his designs in the Netherlands, Philip in 1587 handed over the monopoly to the "Companha Portugueza das Indias Orientas," but such was the ferment caused at Goa by this transaction that the Company soon ceased to exist. The next viceroy was Mathias de Albuquerque, who returned from Portugal in 1591, in which year Fitch reached home.

As already stated, the influence of the Portuguese, and also their trading stations, extended to other regions further east, but a characteristic of their enterprise in these parts appears in the fact that the adventurers rarely established themselves beyond the coast line. Perhaps the most conspicuous exception to this rule is presented in the district of St. Thomé, Southern India. Here the Portuguese discovered a branch of the Christian Church actually established, the question as to who founded it being still a matter of discussion, the honour being variously attributed to the apostles SS. Thomas and Bartholomew and others. Sir W. Hunter ("Gazetteer," vol. vi. ch. xi.) deals with this fascinating subject, and points out

[1] Danvers, vol. ii. p. 40.

that "from their first clear emergence into history" the Christians of Southern India belonged to the Syrian or Nestorian rite. Mr. Milne Rae's "Syrian Church in India" (1892) is a further valuable contribution, and the Rev. Alex. D'Orsay, in his curiously interesting work, "Portuguese Discoveries, Dependencies, and Missions" (1893), gives a detailed account of the early relations of the Portuguese with the Christians they found in this corner of the peninsula. Prof. Stephens dates the decline of Portuguese political influence from the death of the Viceroy Dom Joao de Castro at Goa in the arms of his friend St. Francis Xavier in 1548. He adds: "But at the time when the political interest in the career of the Portuguese in Asia diminishes, the religious interest increases. . . . These (missionaries) were the men who made their way into the interior of India, and who penetrated the farthest East." The Inquisition was established at Goa in 1560, but it was not till the seventeenth century that the periodical *auto-da-fé* was commenced. It is of interest to note that the doctrines and ritual of the Nestorians were condemned by the Synod of Diamper (Udayampura) in 1599.

CHAPTER III

HINDUSTAN UNDER AKBAR—FITCH'S NARRATIVE CONTINUED—THREE ENGLISHMEN AT AGRA—TRAVELLERS SEPARATE—A LONELY JOURNEY

AT the time when Master Ralph Fitch and his companions arrived on the shores of India the Moghul Empire was at its zenith. Akbar, son of Humayun and grandson of Baber, the founder of the dynasty, succeeded his father in 1556, being then but fourteen years of age. He came into a heritage of anarchy, and under the tutelage of his guardian, Bairam Khan, the first years of his reign were spent in a desperate struggle with the Afghan power in Hindustan. At the age of eighteen Akbar declared himself Padishah, and set to work systematically to recover such fortresses as remained in the hands of the Afghans, and to subdue the various sultans who ruled over the independent kingdoms which had been carved out of the ruins of the old Delhi Empire. Conquest, rebellion, and reconquest followed till the Great Moghul's dominions extended from Guzerat on the west to Bengal on the east, and included Kabul and Kashmir on the north, and the northern half of the Dekhan in the south.

AKBAR, THE GREAT MOGHUL.

Akbar the reformer.

But besides being a warrior from his youth up, Akbar was a statesman of the highest rank. It has been suggested that he soon discovered how much the Muhammadan religion had lost its force as a power to bind the empire together. Imbued with the religious toleration of his ancestor Chenghiz Khan, he decided upon the revolutionary policy of equality of race and religion as the only possible means of consolidation. With this object in view, we find him, for example, winning over the warlike princes of Rajputana, partly by force, partly by diplomatic marriages and other concessions, till at last he had succeeded in establishing two aristocracies and two armies—one Moghul and Mussulman, the other Rajput and Hindu, either of which was ready to fight rebellious partisans of the opposite race and creed. During all this period Akbar was professedly a Muhammadan, but his wives were allowed to introduce idols into the zenana and to listen to the Brahmin priests. Encouraged by a young and ambitious scholar, one Abul Fazl, whose singular history—rise, prosperity, and death—breathes the true spirit of Eastern legend, the emperor resolved that he alone should be considered the authority in all religious matters. Probably this idea found its root in the fact that all pious Muhammadans were looking for the appearance of a new prophet A.D. 1591–2, being a thousand years from the Hejira. At any rate Akbar broke the power of the ulemas and welcomed the teachers of other religions to his court, inviting priests from Goa, and permitting the establishment of a Roman Catholic church at Agra. In view of these magnanimous impulses, amid an ocean of fanaticism and exotic religions, it is pitiable to record the fact that such a potentate, still under the influence of Abul Fazl, decided to found a new religious system called the Divine Faith, and permitted himself to be worshipped as a type of royalty emanating from God. But his ideas of equality were not limited to these matters, much as they moved the masses. Akbar sought to better his subjects by various methods of reform; he permitted the use of wine, Muhammadanism notwithstanding, but punished intoxication; he endeavoured to put an end to suttee; he raised the age of marriage, and tried to check polygamy; he introduced a land settlement. His latter years were marred by the rebellion of his son Selim, afterwards known as Jehangir, the outbreak, which involved the assassination of Abul Fazl, being ostensibly a Muhammadan rising against Akbar's apostasy. After its suppression the emperor became a changed man and returned to the observances of the faith. He died in 1605, aged sixty-four years, not without suspicion that he had been poisoned at the instigation of his son, who reigned in his stead.[1]

[1] The late Mr. J. Talboys Wheeler's "Short History of India" (Macmillan, 1880). The Rev. Francis Goldie, S.J., in his "First Christian Mission to the Great Mogul" (Dublin, 1897), states that the Akbar in 1579 applied to the Viceroy, the Archbishop of Goa, and the Provincial of the Jesuits for "two learned Fathers and the books of the Law," and that the choice fell upon Fathers Acquaviva and Anthony Montserrat, with Father Henriquez, a Muhammadan convert of Ormuz, as interpreter; they started from Surat in January, 1580. Seven years

An opportune moment.

Fitch and his companions could not have penetrated to the heart of India at a more opportune time, for by 1585, when the Great Moghul had been some thirty years on the throne, the central power had been more or less firmly established. There is something striking in the reflection that it was during the reign of perhaps the most liberal and intellectually brilliant personality ever seen on the throne of Hindustan, and at a period of our own history which all Englishmen are proud to recall, that our first embassy—as represented by Fitch and his fellow travellers, armed with the Queen's letter—to the chief potentate in all India should have reached its destination. Elizabeth died in 1603 and Akbar in 1605, but before either of these dates the systematic attempt to open up trade by the establishment of the East India Company had been launched. Further, at the end of the sixteenth century, history tells us, Akbar, in a spirit not the less magnanimous because it was crude, was trying to rule his empire on principles founded on the welfare of the vast aggregate of his peoples; at the end of the nineteenth century the Queen-Empress of England and India, in more enlightened because more modern fashion, is engaged in the same task, but over a still wider area, in the same land.

earlier (1573), the Viceroy, Antony Moronha, had sent Antony Cabral to Akbar to obtain a treaty for the security of Daman, consequent upon the Emperor's successes in Guzerat. It is further stated, adds Hunter, that one of Akbar's wives was a Christian, and that he ordered his son Murad, when a child, to take "lessons" in Christianity.

Unfortunately we have no details of the reception accorded by Akbar to his English visitors in the narrative which is here continued. Probably Fitch, even after his return to England, still hoped that something would be heard of Newberie, whose privilege and duty it was, as leader of the expedition, to report to the highest authority in the land on the reception of the Queen's letter. Still he tells us enough to show that he and his associates were well treated and enjoyed perfect liberty. In the endeavour to trace each stage of the journey through India, the author again acknowledges with gratitude the invaluable assistance he has obtained from Sir W. Hunter's unparalleled "Gazetteer" (H.). The line of route followed by the travellers after leaving Golconda is somewhat uncertain; probably they joined various trading caravans and pursued well-defined trade routes. We have had one or two glimpses of their traffickings *en route*, and no doubt they adopted the methods of the old merchant-venturers and, at least, met their current expenses in this manner. But after the hurry of the escape their first objective was the court of Akbar, at Agra or Fatehpur Sikri. In the attempts to identify the places mentioned by Fitch under the old names the latitude and longitude are given to assist the judgment of the reader :—

INDIA—THE JOURNEY (SECOND PART).

Bellergan a towne.

"One of the first townes which we came vnto, is called Bellergan,[1] where there is a great market kept of Dia-

[1] Belgaum.

mants, Rubies, Saphires, and many other soft stones. From Bellergan we went to Bisapor[1] which is a very great towne where the king doeth keepe his court. Hee hath many Gentiles in his court and they bee great idolaters. And they haue their idols standing in the Woods, which they call Pagodes. Some bee like a Cowe, some like a Monkie, some like Buffles, some like peacockes, and some like the deuill. Here be very many elephants which they goe to warre withall. Here they haue good store of gold and siluer: their houses are of stone very faire and high. From hence wee went for Gulconda, the king whereof is called Cutup de lashach.[2] Here and in the kingdome of Hidalcan, and in the countrey of the king of Decan bee the Diamants found of the olde water.[3] It is a very

Bisapor.

Gulconda.

[1] Bijapur.

[2] Possibly (as Mr. W. Foster suggests), Muhammad Kuli Kutb Shah, who reigned from 1580. Golconda, now a fortress and ruined city of the Nizam's dominions, seven miles west of Hyderabad. "The diamonds of Golconda have obtained great celebrity throughout the world; but they were merely cut and polished here, being generally found at Partial" (H.).

[3] See Linschoten's statement that the "principall intent" of the English travellers was to purchase precious stones. It will have been noted that Fitch also makes special reference to the "round and Orient" pearls of Bahrein island; but it cannot be doubted that far larger motives prompted and sustained the adventurers.

faire towne, pleasant, with faire houses of bricke and timber, it aboundeth with great store of fruites and fresh water. Here the men and the women do go with a cloth bound round their middles without any more apparell. We found it here very hote.

Masulipatan. "The winter beginneth here about the last of May. In these partes is a porte or hauen called Masulipatan, which standeth eight dayes iourney from hence toward the gulfe of Bengala, whether come many shippes out of India, Pegu, and Sumatra, very richly laden with Pepper, spices, and other commodities.[1] The countrie is very good and fruitfull. From thence Seruidore. I went to Seruidore which is a fine countrey, and the king is called, the king of Bread. The houses here bee all thatched and made of lome. Here be many Moores and Gentiles, but there is small religion among them. Bellapore. From thence I went to Bellapore,[2]

[1] Masulipatam was the earliest British settlement on the Coromandel coast. An agency was established in 1611 by Capt. Hippon, who commanded the *Globe* in the East India Company's seventh voyage. In 1632 the English were granted a farman by the Muhammadan King of Golconda, which is known as the "Golden Firman" (H.).

[2] Balapur, in the Akola District, Berar, lat. 20° 40′ N., long. 76° 49′ 15″ E. A great fair was formerly held here. The Jama Masjid, now a ruin, bears date 1032 A. H. (Ibid.).

and so to Barrampore,[1] which is in the country of Zelabdim Echebar. In this place their money is made of kind of siluer round and thicke, to the value of twentie pence, which is very good siluer. It is marueilous great and a populous countrey. In their winter which is in Iune, Iuly, and August, there is no passing in the streetes but with horses, the waters be so high. The houses are made of lome and thatched. Here is great store of cotton cloth made, and painted clothes of cotton wooll: here groweth great store of corne and Rice. We found mariages great store both in townes and villages in many places where wee passed, of boyes of eight or ten yeeres, and girls of fiue or six yeeres old. They both do ride vpon one horse very trimly decked, and are caried through the towne with great piping and playing, and so returne

Strange mariages.

[1] Burhanpur, a town in the Nimar District, Central Provinces. Lat. 21° 18′ 33″ N., long. 76° 16′ 26″ E. Founded in 1400 by Nasir Khan: eleven princes of the Farukhi dynasty of Khandesh held Burhanpur till the kingdom was annexed by Akbar, which did not take place, however, till 1600. The *Ain-i-Akbari*, which describes the place as a large city, says, "In the summer the town is covered with dust, and during the rains the streets are full of mud and stone" (Ibid.).

home and eate of a banket made of Rice and fruits, and there they daunce the most part of the night and so make an ende of the marriage. They lie not together vntill they be ten yeeres old. They say they marry their children so yoong, because it is an order that when the man dieth, the woman must be burned with him: so that if the father die, yet they may haue a father in lawe to helpe to bring vp the children which bee maried: and also that they will not leaue their sonnes without wiues, nor their daughters without husbands. From thence we went to

Mandoway a very strong town.

Mandoway, which is a very strong towne. It was besieged twelue yeeres by Zelabdim Echebar before hee could winne it. It standeth vpon a very great high rocke as the most part of their castles doe, and was of a very great circuite.[1] From hence wee went to

[1] Mandoway, Mandogarh (Mandu), which would lie on the route followed, assumedly, by the three travellers, is now a deserted town in Dhar State, Central India, but was formerly the capital of the Muhammadan kingdom of Malwa. Lat. 22° 21′ N., long. 75° 26′ E., and thirty miles S.W. from Mhow. The city, 1,944 ft. above sea-level, occupies eight miles of ground, extending along the crest of the Vindhyas; and is separated from the tableland, with which it is on a level, by a valley which is 300 to 400 yds. broad and about 300 ft. deep. Akbar captured the city in 1570 (H.).

Vgini.

Vgini[1] and Serringe,[2] where wee ouertooke the ambassadour of Zelabdim Echebar with a marueilous great company of men, elephants, and camels. Here is great trade of cotton and cloth made of cotton, and great store of drugs.

Agra a great citie.

"From thence we went to Agra passing many riuers, which by reason of the raine were so swollen, that wee waded and swamme oftentimes for our liues. Agra is a very great citie and populous, built with stone, hauing faire and large streetes, with a faire riuer running by it, which falleth into the gulfe of Bengala. It hath a faire castle and a strong with a very faire ditch. Here bee many Moores and Gentiles, the king is called Zelabdim Echebar: the people for the most part call him The great Mogor. From thence wee went for Fatepore, which is the place where the king

The great Mogor.

[1] Ujjain (Ujjaiyini), a town in the native state of Gwalior, lat. 23° 11′ 10″ N., and long. 75° 51′ 45″ E.; in ancient times the famous capital of Malwa, one of the seven sacred cities of the Hindus, and the spot which marked the first meridian of Hindu geographers. In 1571 the whole of this part of India was conquered by Akbar. The ruins of the ancient city are about a mile to the northward of the present site (H.).

[2] Sironji in Tonk State, Rajputana; lat. 24° 6′ 23″ N., long. 77° 43′ 30″ E., about 140 miles N.E. of Ujjain. It was once a large town famed for its muslins and chintzes (Ibid.).

kept his court.[1] The towne is greater than Agra, but the houses and streetes be not so faire. Here dwell many people both Moores and Gentiles. The king hath in Agra and Fatepore as they doe credibly report 1,000. elephants, thirtie thousand horses, 1,400. tame Deere, 800. concubines: such store of Ounces, Tigers, Buffles, Cocks & Haukes, that is very strange to see. He keepeth a great court, which they call Dericcan.[2] Agra and Fatepore are two very great cities, either of them much greater than London and very populous. Betweene Agra and Fatepore are 12. miles, and all the way is a market of victuals & other things, as full as though a man were still in a towne, and so many people as if a man were in a market. They haue many fine cartes,

The like is reported of the cities of China.

[1] Agra, lat. 27° 10′ 6″ N., long. 78° 5′ 4″ E. Akbar had fixed his seat of government at the present Agra, which he founded on the right bank of the Jumna in 1566, in preference to Delhi, where his father Humayun held his court. In 1570 he laid the foundations of Fatehpur Sikri with the intention of constituting that town the capital of his empire, but was dissuaded, it is suggested, by the better situation of Agra on the river. Fatehpur Sikri, says the *Ain-i-Akbari*, was in 1596 a rendezvous of merchants from all the known quarters of the globe; at the present day it chiefly consists of an expanse of ruins, enclosed in a high stone wall about five miles in circumference (H.). Fitch draws a lively picture of this busy centre of Moghul power as he saw it.

[2] Probably Dera-i-Khan, house of the prince.

and many of them carued and gilded with gold, with two wheeles which be drawen with two litle Buls about the bignesse of our great dogs in England, and they will runne with any horse, and carie two or three men in one of these cartes: they are couered with silke or very fine cloth, and be vsed here as our Coches be in England. Hither is great resort of marchants from Persia and out of India, and very much marchandise of silke and cloth, and of precious stones, both Rubies, Diamants, and Pearles. The king is apparelled in a white Cabie made like a shirt tied with strings on the one side, and a litle cloth on his head coloured oftentimes with red or yealow. None come into his house but his eunuches which keepe his women.

"Here in Fatepore we staied all three vntill the 28. of September 1585, and then master Iohn Newberie tooke his journey toward the citie of Lahor, determining from thence to goe for Persia and then for Aleppo or Constantinople, whether hee could get soonest passage vnto, and directed me to goe for Bengala and for Pegu, and did promise me, if it pleased God, to meete me in Bengala within two yeeres with a shippe out of England. I left William

Wil. Leades serued the king of Cambaia.

Leades the ieweller in seruice with the king Zelabdim Echebar in Fatepore, who did entertaine him very well, and gaue him an house and fiue slaues, an horse, and euery day sixe S. S. in money.[1]

"I went from Agra to Satagam in Bengala, in the companie of one hundred and fourescore boates laden with Salt, Opium, Hinge, Lead, Carpets, and diuers other commodities downe the riuer Iemena.[2] The chiefe marchants are Moores and Gentiles. In these countries they haue many strange ceremonies. The Bramanes which are their priests, come to the water and haue a string about their necks made with great ceremonies, and lade vp water with both their hands, and turne the string first with both their hands within, and then one arme after the other out. Though it be neuer so cold, they will wash themselues in cold water or in warme. These Gentiles will eate no flesh nor kill any thing. They liue with rice, butter, milke, and fruits.

The superstitious ceremonies of the Bramanes.

[1] As already stated Newberie was never heard of again, nor does Leedes appear to have found his way home.

[2] Down the rivers Jumna and Ganges to Satgaon (or Saptagram), now a ruined town in the Hugli District, but sometime the mercantile capital of Bengal. Lat. 22° 38′ 20″ N., long. 88° 25′ 10″ E. (H.).

They pray in the water naked, and dresse their meat & eate it naked, and for their penance they lie flat vpon the earth, and rise vp and turne themselues about 30. or 40. times, and vse to heaue vp their hands to the sunne, & to kisse the earth, with their armes and legs stretched along out, and their right leg always before the left. Euery time they lie downe, they make a score on the ground with their finger to know when their stint is finished. The Bramanes marke themselues in the foreheads, eares and throates with a kind of yellow geare which they grind, & euery morning they do it. And they haue some old men which go in the streetes with a boxe of yellow pouder, and marke men on their heads & necks as they meet them. And their wiues do come by 10. 20. & 30. together to the water side singing, & there do wash themselues, & then vse their ceremonies, & marke themselues in their foreheds and faces, and cary some with them, and so depart singing. Their daughters be maried, at, or before the age of 10. yeres. Their men may haue 7. wiues. They be a kind of craftie people, worse then the Jewes. When they salute one another, they heaue vp their hands to their heads, and say Rame,

Rame.[1] Frō Agra I came to Prage, where the riuer Iemena entreth into the mightie riuer Ganges, and Iemena looseth his name.[2] Ganges cometh out of the Northwest, & runneth East into the gulfe of Bengala. In those parts there are many Tigers and many partriges & turtle doues, and much other foule. Here be many beggers in these countries which goe naked, and the people make great account of them : they call them Schesche. Here I sawe one which was a monster among the rest. He would haue nothing vpon him, his beard was very long, and with the haire of his head he couered his priuities. The nailes of some of his fingers were two inches long, for he would cut nothing from him, neither would he speake. He was accompanied with eight or tenne, and they spake for him. When any man spake to him, he would lay his hand upon his brest and bowe himselfe, but would not speake. Hee would not speake to the king. We went from Prage downe Ganges, the which is here very broad. Here is great store of fish

Ganges.

[1] "Ram-Ram ! The commonest salutation between two Hindus meeting on the road ; an invocation of the Divinity" (Yule & Burrell's Anglo-Indian Glossary).

[2] Prage=Prayag, ancient name for Allahabad, by which the city is still known amongst the Hindu population (H.).

of sundry sorts, & of wild foule, as of swannes, geese, cranes, and many other things. The countrey is very fruitfull and populous. The men for the most part haue their faces shauen, and their heads very long, except some which bee all shauen saue the crowne: and some of them are as though a man should set a dish on their heads, and shaue them round, all but the crowne. In this riuer of Ganges are many Ilands. His water is very sweete and pleasant, and the countrey adioyning very fruitfull.

Bannaras.

"From thence wee went to Bannaras which is a great towne, and great store of cloth is made there of cotton, and Shashes for the Moores.[1] In this place they be all Gentiles, and be the greatest idolaters that euer I sawe. To this towne come the Gentiles on pilgrimage out of farre countreys. Here alongst the waters side bee very many faire houses, and in all of them, or for the most part they haue their images standing, which be euill fauoured, made of stone and wood, some some like lions, leopards, and monkeis, some like men & women, and pecocks, and some like

A pilgrimage of the Gentiles.

[1] Benares, the sacred city of Hinduism, situated on the Ganges about 120 miles below its junction with the Jumna (H.).

the deuil with foure armes and 4. hands. They sit crosse legged, some with one thing in their hands, & some another, & by breake of day and before, there are men & women which come out of the towne and wash thēselues in Ganges. And there are diuers old men which vpon places of earth made for the purpose, sit praying, and they giue the people three or foure strawes, which they take & hold them betweene their fingers when they wash themselues: and some sit to marke them in the foreheads, and they haue in a cloth a little Rice, Barlie, or money, which, when they haue washed themselues, they giue to the old men which sit there praying. Afterwards they go to diuers of their images, & giue them of their sacrifices. And when they giue, the old men say certaine prayers, and then is all holy. And in diuers places there standeth a kind of image which in their language they call Ada. And they haue diuers great stones carued, whereon they poure water, & throw thereupon some rice, wheate, barly, and some other things. This Ada hath foure hands with clawes. Moreouer, they haue a great place made of stone like to a well with steppes to goe downe; wherein the water standeth very foule and stinketh: for the great quantitie of flowers, which continually they throwe into it, doe make it stinke. There be alwayes many people in it: for they say when they wash themselues in it, that their sinnes be forgiuen them, because God, as they say, did wash himselfe in that place. They gather vp the sand in the bottome of it, and say it is holy. They neuer pray but in the water, and they wash themselues ouer-head, and lade vp water with both their handes, and turne themselues about, and then they drinke a litle of the water three times, and so goe to their gods which stand in those houses. Some of them will wash a place which is their length, and then will pray vpon the earth with their armes and legs at length out, and will rise vp and lie downe, and kisse the ground twentie or thirtie times, but they will not stirre their right foote. And some of them will make their ceremonies with fifteene or sixteene pots litle and great, and ring a litle bel when they make their mixtures tenne or twelue times: and they make a circle of water round about their pots and pray, and diuers sit by them, and one that reacheth them their pots: and they say diuers things ouer their pots many times, and when they haue done, they goe to their gods, and strowe their sacrifices which they thinke are very holy, and marke many of them which sit by, in the foreheads, which they take as a great gift. There come fiftie and sometime an hundred together, to wash them in this well, and to offer to these idols.

"They haue in some of these houses their idoles standing, and one sitteth by them in warme weather with a fanne to blowe winde vpon them. And when they see any company comming, they ring a litle bell which hangeth by them, and many giue them their almes, but especially those which come out of the countrey. Many of them are blacke and haue clawes of brasse with long nayles, and some ride vpon peacockes and other foules which be euill fauoured, with long haukes bils, and some like one thing and some another, but none with a good face. Among the rest there is one which they make great account of: for they say hee giueth them all things both foode and apparell, and one sitteth alwayes by him with a fanne to make wind towards him. Here some bee burned to ashes, some scorched in the fire and throwen into the water, and dogges and foxes doe presently eate them. The wiues here doe burne with their husbands when they die, if they will not, their heads be shauen, and neuer any account is made of them afterward. The people goe all naked saue a litle cloth bound about their middle. Their women haue their necks, armes and eares decked with rings of siluer, copper, tinne, and with round hoopes made of Iuorie, adorned with amber stones, and with many agats, and they are marked with a great spot of red in their foreheads, and a stroke of red vp to the crowne, and so it runneth three maner of wayes. In their Winter, which is our May, the men weare quilted gownes of cotton like to our mattraces and quilted caps like to our great Grocers morters, with a slit to looke out at, and so tied downe beneath their eares. If a man or a woman be sicke and like to die, they will lay him before their idols all night, and that shall helpe him or make an ende of him. And if he do not mend that night, his friends will come and sit with him a litle and cry, and afterwards will cary him to the waters side and set him vpon a litle raft made of reeds, and so let him goe downe the riuer. When they be maried the man and the woman come to the water side, and there is an olde man which they call a Bramane, that is, a priest, a cowe, and a calfe, or a cowe with calfe.

Then the man and the woman, cowe and calfe, and the olde man goe into the water together, and they giue the olde man a white cloth of foure yards long, and a basket crosse bound with diuers things in it: the cloth hee laieth vpon the backe of the cowe, and then he taketh the cowe by the ende of the taile, and saieth certain wordes: and she hath a copper or a brasse pot full of water, and the man doeth hold his hand by the olde mans hand, and the wiues hand by her husbands, and all haue the cowe by the taile and they poure water out of the pot vpon the cowes taile, and it runneth through all their hands, and they lade vp water with their handes, and then the olde man doeth tie him and her together by their clothes. Which done, they goe round about the cowe and calfe, and then they giue some what to the poore which be alwayes there, and to the Bramane or priest they give the cowe and calfe, and afterward goe to diuers of their idoles and offer money, and lie downe flat vpon the ground and kisse it diuers times, and then goe their way. Their chiefe idoles be blacke and euill fauoured, their mouthes monstrous, their eares gilded, and full of iewels, their teeth and eyes of gold, siluer and glasse, some hauing

This tying of new maried folks together by the clothes, was vsed by the Mexicans in old time.

one thing in their handes, and some another. You may not come into the house where they stand, with your shooes on. They haue continually lampes burning before them.

Patenaw.

"From Bannaras I went to Patenaw[1] downe the riuer of Ganges: where in the way we passed many faire townes, and a countrey very fruitfull: and many very great riuers doe enter into Ganges; and some of them as great as Ganges, which cause Ganges to bee of a great breadth, and so broad that in the time of raine you cannot see from one side to the other. These Indians when they bee scorched and throwen into the water, the men swimme with their faces downewards, the women with their faces vpwards, I thought they tied something to them to cause them to doe so: but they say no. There be very many thieues in this countrey, which be like to the Arabians: for they have no certaine abode, but are sometime in one place and sometime in another. Here the women bee so decked with siluer and copper, that it is strange to see, they vse no shooes by reason of the rings of siluer and copper which they weare on their toes. Here at Patanaw they finde

[1] Patna, still one of the largest cities in India (H.).

Gold found. gold in this maner. They digge deepe pits in the earth, and wash the earth in great bolles, and therein they finde the gold, and they make the pits round about with bricke, that the earth fall not in. Patenaw is a very long and a great towne. In times past it was a kingdom, but now it is vnder Zelabdim, Echebar the great Mogor. The men are tall and slender, and haue many old folks among them: the houses are simple, made of earth and couered with strawe, the streetes are very large. In this towne there is a trade of cotton, & cloth of cotton, much sugar, which they cary from hence to Bengala and India, very much Opium & other commodities. He that is chiefe here vnder the king is called Tipperdas, and is of great account among the people. Here in Patenau I saw a dissembling prophet which sate vpon an horse in the market place, and made as though he slept, and many of the people came and touched his feete with their hands, and then kissed their hands. They tooke him for a great man, but sure he was a lasie lubber. I left him there sleeping. The people of these countries be much giuen to such prating and dissembling hypocrites.

Tanda in Gouren. "From Patanaw I went to Tanda

which is in the land of Gouren.[1] It hath in times past bene a kingdom, but now is subdued by Zelabdim Echebar. Great trade and traffique is here of cotton, and of cloth of cotton. The people goe naked with a litle cloth bound about their waste. It standeth in the countrey of Bengala. Here be many Tigers, wild Bufs, and great store of wilde foule: they are very great idolaters. Tanda standeth from the riuer Ganges a league, because in times past the riuer flowing over the bankes, in time of raine did drowne the countrey and many villages, and so they do remaine. And the old way which the riuer Ganges was woont to run, remaineth drie, which is the occasion that the citie doeth stand so farre from the water. From Agra down the riuer Iemena, and downe the riuer Ganges, I was fiue moneths comming to Bengala, but it may be sailed in much shorter time.

Couche: this seemeth to be Quichen, accorted by some among the provinces of China.

"I went from Bengala into the country of Couche, which lieth 25. dayes iourny Northwards from Tanda.[2] The king is

[1] Tanda, Tandan, or Tanra, is a petty village in Maldah District, Bengal, but even the site of the ancient town, which became the capital of Bengal after the decadence of Gaur, has not been accurately determined (H.).

[2] Kuch Behar. From the point of view of the explorer this is the most interesting part of the journey. Fitch evidently had

a Gentile, his name is Suckel Counse:[1] his countrey is great, and lieth not far from Cauchin China: for they say they haue pepper from thence. The port is called Cacchegate. All the countrie is set with Bambos or Canes made sharpe at both endes & driuen into the earth, and they can let in the water & drowne the ground aboue knee deepe, so that mē nor horses can passe. They poison all the waters if any wars be. Here they haue much silke & muske, and cloth made of cotton. The people haue eares which be marueilous great of a span long, which they draw out in length by deuises when they be yong. Here they be all Gentiles, and they will kil nothing. They haue hospitals for sheepe, goates, dogs, cats, birds, & for all other liuing creatures. When they be old & lame, they keepe them vntil they die. If a man catch or buy any quicke thing in other places & bring it thither, they will giue

Pure Gentilisina.

an afterthought on the subject, for he refers to it in a subsequent passage in his narrative.

[1] Lieut.-Gen. Fytche in "Burma Past and Present," vol. i. p. 7 (Kegan Paul, 1878), says: "Col. Haughton, late Commissioner of the Cooch Behar Division, has kindly furnished me with a Coorsinamah, or genealogical table of the Cooch Behar family, in which this prince appears under the name of Sukladuge or Seela Roy; he was the progenitor of the Durrung branch of the family."

him mony for it or other victuals, & keepe it in their hospitals or let it go, They will giue meat to the Ants. Their smal mony is almonds, which oftentimes they vse to eat.

In Mexico they vse likes wise for small money the fruit Cacao which are like almonds.

Hugely.

"From thence I returned to Hugeli, which is the place where the Portugals keep in the country of Bengala which standeth in 23. degrees of Northerly latitude, and standeth a league from Satagan: they cal it Porto Piqueno.[1] We went through the wildernes, because the right way was full of thieues, where we passed the countrey of Gouren, where we found but few villages, but almost all wildernes, & saw many buffes, swine & deere, grasse longer then a mã, and very many Tigers. Not far from Porto Piqueno southwestward, standeth an hauen which is called Angeli, in the countrey of Orixa. It was a kingdom of it selfe, & the king was a great friend to strangers. Afterwards it was taken by the king of Patan which was their neighbour, but he did not enjoy it long,

Porto Angeli.

[1] Hugli, now the chief town and administrative headquarters of Hugli District, Bengal, is situated on the east bank of the river of the same name. Lat. 22° 54′ 44″ N., long. 88° 26′ 28″ E. It is said to have been founded by the Portuguese in 1537 on the decay of Satgaon (Fitch's Satagam or Satagan already identified), the royal port of Bengal, caused by the silting up of the Saraswati river (H.).

but was taken by Zelabdim Echebar which is king of Agra, Delli, & Cambaia. Orixa standeth 6 daies iourney from Satagan southwestward.[1] In this place is very much Rice, and cloth made of cotton, & great store of cloth which is made of grasse, which they call Yerua, it is like a silke. They make good cloth of it which they send for India & diuers other places. To this hauen of Angeli come euery yere many ships out of India, Negapatan, Sumatra, Malacca, and diuers other places; & lade from thence great store of Rice, & much cloth of cotton wooll, much sugar, & long pepper, great store of butter & other victuals for India. Satagam is a faire citie for a citie of the Moores, and very plentifull of all things. Here in Bengala they haue euery day in one place or other a great market which they call Chandeau, and they haue many great boats which they cal pericose, wherewithall they go from place to

The like cloth may be made of the long grasse in Virginia.

Satagam.

[1] Orissa, the Holy Land of the Hindus. In 1567-8 Sulaiman, the Afghan king of Bengal, overran Orissa and captured the city of Puri where stands the famous shrine of Jagannath (Vishnu). His second son, Daud Khan, who succeeded to the governorship of Bengal, threw off his allegiance to the Moghul Emperor at Delhi with the result that in 1578 a battle took place in which Daud was killed. Orissa became a province of Akbar's empire, and remained so till 1751, when the Marathas obtained it (H.).

place and buy Rice and many other things: these boates haue 24. or 26. oares to rowe them, they be great of burthen, but haue no couerture. Here the Gentiles haue the water of Ganges in great estimation, for hauing good water neere them, yet they will fetch the water of Ganges a great way off, and if they haue not sufficient to drinke, they will sprinkle a litle on them, and then they thinke themselues well. From Satagam I trauelled by the countrey of the king of Tippara or porto Grande, with whom the Mogores or Mogen haue almost continuall warres. The Mogen which be of the kingdom of Recon and Rame, be stronger then the king of Tippara, so that Chatigan or porto Grande is oftentimes vnder the king of Recon.[1]

Tippara or porto Grande.

[1] At this time, says Sir Arthur Phayre in his "History of Burma," p. 270 (Trübner, 1883), Chittagaon, or Chittagong, was subject to Arakan: "The name of Ramu is applied to the country of Chittagaon in a general description of Bengal which is found in Purchas (vol. v. p. 508). These instances probably explain the name of Ruhmi, Rahma, or Rahmaa given to a kingdom on the sea coast of the Bay of Bengal by the Arabian voyagers in the ninth and tenth centuries of the Christian era. It has been supposed to refer to Ramri in Arakan, or to Ramanya, the classic name of Pegu. There is now a village called Ramu in the southern part of the Chittagaon district, which is a police station. It probably represents the name by which the territory in question was known to the Arabs, and which we may now conclude extended from the north bank of the river Naf to the confines of Bengal. Fitch heard the name

Bottanter a great Northren country. Marchants of China, Moscouia and Tartarie.

"There is a country 4. daies iournie from Couche or Quickeu before mentioned, which is called Bottanter and the citie Bottia, the king is called Dermain; the people whereof are very tall and strong, and there are marchants which come out of China, & they say out of Muscouia or Tartarie. And they come to buy muske, cambals, agats, silke, pepper and saffron like the saffron of Persia. The countrey is very great, 3. moneths iourney. There are very high mountains in this countrey, & one of them so steep that when a man is 6. daies iourney off it, he may see it perfectly. Vpon these mountains are people which haue eares of a spanne long: if their eares be not long, they call them apes. They say that when they be vpon the mountaines, they see ships in the Sea sayling to and fro; but they know

These seeme to be the mountains of Imaus, called by the people Cumao.

when in Chittagaon, and the king of Arakan then held the country north of the Naf." Hunter further states that the district was probably first conquered by the Muhammadans during the period of Afghan supremacy in Bengal, between the thirteenth and sixteenth centuries. During the struggle between the Moghuls and Afghans, towards the close of the sixteenth century, Chittagong seems to have been reconquered by the Raja of Arakan, but the reconquest was ignored by the Moghuls after the final expulsion of the Afghans from Bengal. Todar Mall, Akbar's finance minister in 1582, assessed the place although it was a province of Arakan and remained so till 1666, when it was reannexed to the Moghul empire.

not from whence they come, nor whether they go. There are marchants which come out of the East, they say, from vnder the sunne, which is from China, which haue no beards, and they say there it is something warme. But those which come from the other side of the mountains which is from the North, say there it is very cold. These Northren merchants are apparelled with woollen cloth and hats, white hosen close, and bootes which be of Moscouia or Tartarie. They report that in their countrey they haue very good horses, but they be litle: some men haue foure, fiue, or six hundred horses and kine: they liue with milke and fleshe. They cut the tailes of their kine, and sell them very deere, for they bee in great request, and much esteemed in those partes. The hair of them is a yard long, the rumpe is aboue a spanne long: they vse to hang them for brauerie vpon the heades of their Elephants: they bee much vsed in Pegu and China: they buie and selle by scores vpon the ground. The people be very swift on foote.[1]

The apparel of the Tartarie marchants.

Cowe tailes in great request.

[1] This account of Bhutan and the traffic from beyond the Himalaya—which, confessedly, is all hearsay—gives rise to the suggestion that if Fitch had continued the journey northward from Kuch Behar he would have found no difficulty in entering Tibet. He might even have penetrated to Lhasa, and estab-

"From Chatigan in Bengala, I came

Bacola. to Bacola; the king whereof is a Gentile, a man very well disposed and delighted much to shoot in a gun. His countrey is very great and fruitful, and hath store of Rice, much cotton cloth, and cloth of silke. The houses be very faire and high builded, the streetes large, the people naked, except a litle cloth about their waste. The women weare great store of siluer hoopes about their neckes and armes, and their legs are ringed with siluer and copper, and rings made of elephants teeth.[1]

Serrepore. "From Bacola I went to Serrepore which standeth vpon the riuer of Ganges, the king is called Chondery. They be all hereabouts rebels against their king

lished the record of the first British visitor to that semi-mysterious city which even to this day has only been trodden by one Englishman (Manning, about 1811). The description he gives of the Bhutias as an athletic, vigorous race still holds good, according to Hunter, but they are degraded by mis-government, "their morals are extremely low, and their numbers reduced by the unnatural system of polyandry and the excessive prevalence of monastic institutions." Nominally, there are two supreme authorities, the Dharm Raja, the spiritual head, and the Deb Raja, the temporal ruler.

[1] Probably Barisal, the present headquarters of the Bakarganj district, which is described as "a typical part of the alluvial delta formed by the three great river systems of Bengal." It is further suggested that Bakarganj formed part of Todar Mall's (1582) Sirkar of Sonargaon. The town is situated in lat. 22° 41′ 40″ N., long. 90° 24′ 30″ E. (H.).

Zebaldim Echebar: for here are so many riuers and Ilands, that they flee from one to another, whereby his horsemen cannot preuaile against them. Great store of cotton cloth is made here.[1]

Sinnergan.

"Sinnergan is a towne sixe leagues from Serrepore, where there is the best and finest cloth made of cotton that is in all India. The chiefe king of all these countries is called Isacan, and he is chiefe of all the other kings, and is a great friend to all Christians. The houses here, as they be in the most part of India, are very litle, and couered with strawe, and haue a fewe mats round about the wals, and the doore to keepe out the Tygers and the Foxes. Many of the people are very rich. Here they will eate no flesh, nor kill no beast: They liue of Rice, milke, and fruits. they goe with a litle cloth before them, and all the rest of their bodies is naked. Great store of Cotton cloth goeth from hence, and much Rice, wherewith they serue all India, Ceilon, Pegu, Malacca,

[1] Serampur, chief town of a sub-division of the same name in the Hugli District, Bengal, lat. 22° 45′ 26″ N., and long. 88° 23″ 10″ E. Formerly a Danish Settlement, but ceded to the East India Co. in 1845; famous as the scene of the labours of the Baptist Missionaries—Carey, Marshman, and Ward (H.).

Sumatra, and many other places."[1]

(Continued on page 153.)

[1] Sonargaon, the ancient Muhammadan capital of East Bengal, now an insignificant village called Painam in the Dacca District, lat. 23° 39′ 45″ N., long. 90° 38′ 20″ E. Azim Shah, son of Sikandar, proclaimed his independence here and invited the poet Hafiz to his court. It lies hidden in a grove of palms and bush, and is surrounded by a deep muddy ditch, once a moat (H.). Isa Khan, who was in power when Fitch visited the city, maintained his independent rule for several years, but at his death the district became part of the Moghul Empire. The cloth referred to was the famous Dacca muslin (Cunningham : "India, Archæological Survey Reports," vol. xv. p. 135).

BOOK III

IN THE FURTHER EAST

ALBUQUERQUE.

CHAPTER I

BURMA AND MALACCA—RISE OF AN EMPIRE—PORTUGUESE ADVENTURERS

THE third and final stage of Ralph Fitch's journeyings before he set his face homeward was to the confines of Portuguese authority. Possibly if Newberie had continued eastward some attempt would have been made to carry the Queen's letter to the Chinese Emperor; Fitch, however, not only proceeded to Pegu but went on to Malacca and thus reached the furthest centre, but one, under European government. The risks he ran in this unsettled region, where the Western adventurers were already not too favourably known, were perhaps less on the whole than on the Malabar Coast, where Portuguese jealousy was added to native suspicion and Mussulman rivalry. It is possible in these days to realise somewhat of the attractions which would have tempted him to brave even greater dangers. The reports of the glories of Pegu rivalled those of Golden Goa, and as Fitch came nearer to the city he must have heard still more of them. This was the heyday of the Burmese renaissance, and the great wealth accumulated in the sea-ports was overflowing for the benefit of all comers, for there seems to have been considerable freedom in trade. Even where commerce became hampered by the wars of the local kings along the coast-line from Arakan on the west to Siam on the east, the services of the European visitors were eagerly enlisted. The Portuguese utterly failed to obtain anything approaching permanent influence of importance anywhere on the coasts beyond their emporium at Malacca, and do not appear to have attempted seriously to secure it. The following is a short account of the rise of their dominion, such as it was, in these distant seas, and an historical summary of events in the adjoining empire, immediately prior to and including the period of the visit of the first Englishman to Burma—a record which is rich in stirring episodes:

Capture of Malacca.

Albuquerque having established himself at Goa (November, 1510) threw his powerful energies into the task of extending his country's influence further east. Malacca, the gate to the Spice Islands, was his first objective, the ostensible reason for his attack on the flourishing city being the treachery of the Muhammadan Sultan. The first European fleet to visit this important emporium arrived in 1509 under Diogo Lopes de Sequeira, who came with five ships, one of his companions being Ruy de Araujo, a friend and supporter of Albuquerque, who had not yet succeeded to the Governorship of India. Hearing of a plot to murder the Portuguese and destroy their vessels—organised by their old rivals the Muhammadan traders—Sequeira burnt two of his ships and sailed away with the other three, leaving Araujo, who had been landed as factor, and his staff of about twenty Portuguese to their fate. To wreak vengeance on the Sultan of Malacca a squadron of four sail was despatched from Portugal in 1510 under the command of Diogo Mendes de Vasconcellos, but was detained by Albuquerque to assist in the operations at Goa. These having been carried out with distinguished success the latter, who was now Governor, determined to plant Portuguese power once for all in the Eastern gate. At this time it is recorded that Malacca had 100,000 inhabitants, and such was the representation of the various races that four special Captains of the Port were appointed to rule the chief nationalities, Chinese, Javanese, Guzeratis and Bengalis respectively; the Sultan was of Javanese extraction.

Sailing with a force of eighteen vessels and 1,400 men, Albuquerque touched at Pedir in Sumatra in May, 1511, having lost one galley in the run from Goa. Here he found nine of the Portuguese prisoners who had effected their escape, and who no doubt were of great assistance to him in his design upon the populous city. On arriving at Malacca some time was spent in fruitless negotiations with the Sultan for the release of Araujo and his remaining companions, till at last a letter was received from the imprisoned factor, who, with rare fidelity to the cause of his country, urged Albuquerque to disregard his fate and to attack the city at once. To bring matters to a crisis boats were sent from the fleet to fire the ships in the harbour and also the waterside houses, with the result that the Sultan immediately released Araujo and his fellow prisoners—and sealed his own fate. Acting under a plan devised by the newly liberated factor, who, it will be remembered, had spent nearly two years in the city, the first attack was delivered on July 25th, with such success that a second attack, which promptly followed, resulted in the capture of the great city and the expulsion of the Sultan.

A trade centre. Siam, China, and Burma.

Besides setting to work at once to build a permanent fort at Malacca, Albuquerque, with the statesmanlike sagacity which distinguished the whole of his career as Governor, took steps to preserve the reputation of the city as a great *entrepôt*. Certain Chinese traders and sailors, who were protected by him during the assaults, returned home in their own junks, full of stories of his prowess and magnanimity, with the result that the deposed Sultan could obtain no help from that quarter. A Hindu merchant, who had befriended Araujo during his captivity, found that his property was respected, a fact which won over the representatives of that section of the polyglot city. The Burmese and other foreign traders were also encouraged, but, on the other hand, the Malay Mussulmans were given no mercy, and were cowed to begin with by the public execution of a leading Javanese merchant for an act of treachery.

In carrying out his great ideal Albuquerque sent emissaries in various directions to reach the sources of trade supplies. One of these was Duarte Fernandes, who proceeded to Siam with the Chinese junks and established very cordial relations with the king. Messages were also received by the new conqueror from the King of Campar (? Champa, Cochin China), the son-in-law of the late King of Malacca, and the King of Java, while a trading mission in the shape of three large rowing-boats came in from Menecambo at the southern point of Sumatra. Albuquerque responded amicably to all these advances, and the messengers were sent back loaded with gifts in exchange for the presents they brought; Antonia de Miranda de Azevedo being despatched as special ambassador to Siam. One of the most important of his missions, intended to consolidate the trade relations of the new eastern metropolis, was that of Antonio de Abreu, who, in command of three ships, was ordered to explore the Moluccas and the region of the Spice Islands generally. In this expedition, it is interesting to note, there sailed a young Portuguese gentleman, Fernao de Magalhaes, who, as Magellan, has left his name on the map of the world.[1] Duarte Coelho was sent to Cochin China and Tongking, and Ruy Nunez d'Acunha to Pegu. Having made these arrangements and provided for the administration of Malacca during his absence, the Governor returned to Goa, narrowly escaping death from shipwreck on the way. He found his Indian metropolis again invested by an army from Bijapur,

[1] Stephens, p. 109. Danvers (vol i. chap. viii.) gives the names of de Abreu's companions as Francisco Serrao and Simao Affonso; probably they had command of two of the vessels.

strengthened by deserters from his own garrison, for even thus early Portuguese freebooters and renegades began to figure prominently in these parts. The relief of Goa was carried through in brilliant fashion (1512), and Rasul Khan, having been in turn invested in the fortress of Benasterim, at length capitulated. The terms of surrender were that the deserters should be given up, on condition that their lives were spared, and that the rest of the forces should be allowed to march out minus their stores, horses, and artillery. Albuquerque, with all the savagery of his time, kept his word as regards sparing the lives of the renegades, but mutilated them in a shocking manner. After cutting off their ears and noses, their right hands and thumbs of their left hands, he shipped them to Portugal as a warning to other adventurers who were crowding the Indian fleets. The old chronicler (Sousa) tells us that one of these maimed and disfigured wretches, Ferdinando Lopez, voluntarily stayed "with a black" in the Island of St. Helena, where he afterwards proved serviceable to passing caravels.

The first systematic attempt to dominate the trade of the Further East from its principal centre, Malacca, proved more or less successful for many years. Thus King Sebastian of Portugal divided the eastern governorship into three parts, and in 1571 the next Viceroy, Don Antonio de Noronha, found that he was to be supreme only from the coasts of Arabia to Ceylon, with his capital at Goa, to control the Indian and Persian trade. Another Governor, with headquarters at Malacca, was appointed for the spice trade, with jurisdiction from Bengal to the Furthest East; and a third to rule all the Portuguese settlements on the south-east coast of Africa, with his capital at Mozambique.

First traffic with Burma. "A pious fraud."

Up to the time of Fitch's wanderings in these regions, the Portuguese had only succeeded in founding one or two temporary settlements upon what we now know as the Burmese coasts. Indeed, with the exception of an occasional friendly trade treaty, their political connection with this rich country was in the main limited, even in subsequent years, to the doubtful advantages arising from the exploits of their own unruly soldiers of fortune. The rich metropolitan city and port of Pegu was well known, at least by repute, in Albuquerque's time, and we are told that in his operations at Malacca he was assisted by three hundred men belonging to the merchants of the city.[1] No account appears to have been preserved of the mission of Ruy Nunez d'Acunha to the capital. In 1517 John de Silveira, who had been sent to the Maldives to obtain permission to build a fort, returned to Goa with four sail. He had accomplished his task, but during the voyage seized two vessels belonging to Cambay and sent them to Cochin as prizes. This high-handed act did not pass unnoticed by a member of his crew, described as "a young Bengalian." Silveira was next despatched to Chittagong, but as the event proved the Portuguese could hardly have chosen a worse representative to obtain for them a footing in a new country. The "young Bengalian"

[1] Sousa, vol. i. p. 181.

told his story and denounced Silveira as a pirate. "It had been worse with him," says Sousa, "had not John Coello arrived there with his ship from Pacem, being sent on the same errand by Ferdinando Perez de Andrade to the King of Bengala." Silveira passed the winter with great hardship, for the people of the country would have nothing to do with him. Chittagong at this time was subject to Arakan, and, on the baffled treaty-maker preparing to leave the king sent him a present and invited him ashore. Silveira, however, shrewdly guessed what was in store for him, and continued his return voyage till he reached Ceylon, where he eventually became Governor of the settlement. Thus inauspiciously ended the first recorded story of Portuguese communication with the western portion of the Burmese coast, the nature of it being but a type of what was to follow, for the Sunderbunds in after years became a nest of pirates. In 1518 Lopo Soarez de Albergaria was succeeded in the Governorship by Diogo Lopes de Sequiera, to whom we are told "the King gave the Government of India as a reward of his good service in Africk, his discovery of Malaca and worthy Qualities."[1]

[1] Sousa, vol. i. p. 224, states that Sequiera left Lisbon with nine ships and 1,500 fighting-men, adding: "At the Cape of Good Hope, one Ship was in danger of perishing by means of a great fish, which running against her, stuck the length of two spans of a long Beak it has into her side; this was afterwards found to be the Fish called the '*Needle*.'" We have already witnessed an exhibition of Sequeira's "worthy qualities" at Malacca in 1509, when he appears to have made no effort to rescue Araujo and his companions.

In the following year (1519) Andrea Correa arrived at Malacca, having been more successful in establishing relations with another portion of Burma than Silveira had proved with the potentate of Arakan. Correa's expedition was to Martaban, which had become a great port, especially since the Cape trade had been opened. A populous city (though in recent times only the size of a village) seated at the mouth of the Salwin river, it was governed by a Viceroy who had control of a large extent of territory, and held great state.[1] Correa reported that he had concluded a treaty with the King of Pegu's Viceroy, and the following amusing account of the ceremony is given by Sousa:—

"At the swearing of the Peace assisted with the King's Ministers, the Priests of both Nations, Catholick and Gentiles. The Heathen was called the Great *Raulim*, who after the Capitulations made in the Golden Mine, as is the Custom of those People were publickly read, began to read in a Book, and then taking some yellow Paper (a colour dedicated to their holy uses) with some sweet Leaves of Trees, whereon were certain Characters, set Fire to it all, and then taking the Hands of the King's Minister and holding them over the ashes, said some words, which rendered the Oath inviolable. Anthony Correa, to answer this Solemnity, ordered his Priest to put on a Surplice and bring his Breviary, which was so tottered and torn, that it was scandalous those Heathens should see how little respect was paid to our sacred Books. Correa observing this, ordered to be brought instead of it a Book of Church-

[1] Phayre, p. 96, says the Viceroy was styled Soabinya, and that he was the brother-in-law of the King of Pegu.

by their old rivals the Muhammadan traders—Sequeira burnt two of his ships and sailed away with the other three, leaving Araujo, who had been landed as factor, and his staff of about twenty Portuguese to their fate. To wreak vengeance on the Sultan of Malacca a squadron of four sail was despatched from Portugal in 1510 under the command of Diogo Mendes de Vasconcellos, but was detained by Albuquerque to assist in the operations at Goa. These having been carried out with distinguished success the latter, who was now Governor, determined to plant Portuguese power once for all in the Eastern gate. At this time it is recorded that Malacca had 100,000 inhabitants, and such was the representation of the various races that four special Captains of the Port were appointed to rule the chief nationalities, Chinese, Javanese, Guzeratis and Bengalis respectively; the Sultan was of Javanese extraction.

Sailing with a force of eighteen vessels and 1,400 men, Albuquerque touched at Pedir in Sumatra in May, 1511, having lost one galley in the run from Goa. Here he found nine of the Portuguese prisoners who had effected their escape, and who no doubt were of great assistance to him in his design upon the populous city. On arriving at Malacca some time was spent in fruitless negotiations with the Sultan for the release of Araujo and his remaining companions, till at last a letter was received from the imprisoned factor, who, with rare fidelity to the cause of his country, urged Albuquerque to disregard his fate and to attack the city at once. To bring matters to a crisis boats were sent from the fleet to fire the ships in the harbour and also the waterside houses, with the result that the Sultan immediately released Araujo and his fellow prisoners—and sealed his own fate. Acting under a plan devised by the newly liberated factor, who, it will be remembered, had spent nearly two years in the city, the first attack was delivered on July 25th, with such success that a second attack, which promptly followed, resulted in the capture of the great city and the expulsion of the Sultan.

A trade centre. Siam, China, and Burma.

Besides setting to work at once to build a permanent fort at Malacca, Albuquerque, with the statesmanlike sagacity which distinguished the whole of his career as Governor, took steps to preserve the reputation of the city as a great *entrepôt*. Certain Chinese traders and sailors, who were protected by him during the assaults, returned home in their own junks, full of stories of his prowess and magnanimity, with the result that the deposed Sultan could obtain no help from that quarter. A Hindu merchant, who had befriended Araujo during his captivity, found that his property was respected, a fact which won over the representatives of that section of the polyglot city. The Burmese and other foreign traders were also encouraged, but, on the other hand, the Malay Mussulmans were given no mercy, and were cowed to begin with by the public execution of a leading Javanese merchant for an act of treachery.

In carrying out his great ideal Albuquerque sent emissaries in various directions to reach the sources of trade supplies. One of these was Duarte Fer-

who treasured the memories of the old empire; the Burmese nobles who resented the rule of the Shans found an asylum among the hills of Taungu, and persecution drove Buddhist monks thither from Ava. That Kyinyo cherished some design to restore the Burmese dynasty, in name at least, appears to be reflected in the fact that the Burmese chronicles trace his descent from the last King of Pagan. In 1530 he was succeeded by his son Mengtara, or Tabeng Shwehti, who entered upon his father's great project with all the ardour of a youth of sixteen—at a time, too, when surrounding circumstances appeared to afford every opportunity for a scheme of restoration. In Pegu a king known as Binya Ran had concluded a long and comparatively peaceful reign of thirty-five years. It is recorded as remarkable that he only marched out of his dominions at the head of an army on two occasions, and one of these is described as a pilgrimage. The other expedition, however, which was an unsuccessful attempt to crush the rising state of Taungu—the home of the refugee—sowed the seeds of retaliation in fruitful ground. Binya Ran, whose glories are recorded by early European travellers, died in 1526, and was succeeded in his possessions, which included the Viceroyalty of Martaban under Soabinya, by his son Takarwutbi, who was then fifteen years of age. As to the other neighbouring kingdoms, Prome had become involved in the disputes of the Shan chiefs who rapidly followed each other on the throne of Ava, and about the time that Tabeng succeeded his father in Taungu, the government of Prome had just been seized by one Narabadi.

In Arakan a young king of considerable ability, and known as Meng Beng, was reigning, his territories including Chittagong. As to the shattered kingdom of Ava, Thohanbwa, son of a Shan chief of Monyin, was at last placed on the throne by his father, and appears to have been mainly distinguished for his hatred to the Burmese race.

Such were Tabeng's neighbours, and, potentially, his rivals and opponents. From the first the young king acted with extraordinary forethought, and from the time he came to the throne he was guided by the wise counsels of his brother-in-law, a very remarkable man whose title, Bureng Naung, subsequently became celebrated in the Portuguese annals, and among the adventurers who served under or against him, as Branginoco. Four or more years were spent in preparing a plan of campaign, and at last it was decided to commence operations by an attack upon the most formidable neighbour of all, the great kingdom of the delta, Pegu.[1]

Fall of Pegu. First Portuguese mercenaries.

When the Burmese forces, with probably a large contingent of Karen auxiliaries from the mountains, marched upon the capital city of Pegu (1534–5), Tabeng Shwehti was not more than twenty-one years of age. He had thus early given promise of unwonted ability, and now appeared as the fitting representative of a hopeful cause. On the other hand, the young king of Pegu, Takarwutbi, during his reign of eight or nine years had given himself up to the pleasures and vices of a rich oriental court.

[1] Phayre, pp. 93–4.

The result of such a conflict, in the days when princes were leaders of armies, was a foregone conclusion. In the first attack Tabeng was beaten back by the Talaings, who were under the generalship not of their king, but of two Shan nobles. Undaunted by this reverse, and unpunished by a counter attack, as they certainly would have been by the late king, Binya Ran, the invaders reappeared before the capital the following year. By this time, it seems, Takarwutbi had secured other foreign aid, for the walls were successfully defended by Indian Mussulman gunners. For a third time (1539) Tabeng invested the city, coming with an enormous force by the Sitang river and by land. How long the siege lasted does not appear, but that the Peguan king was sorely pressed is shown by the eagerness with which he hailed the first recorded appearance of the Portuguese at his capital. He knew something of the white strangers, at all events by repute, for it will be remembered that Soabinya, who was still Viceroy of Martaban, had made a treaty with them some twenty years before, and probably trading relations had been opened up with the greater port. Indeed it was for commercial purposes, ostensibly at least, that they now appeared on the scene. The following is the Portuguese account of what happened:—

"The Viceroy sent Ferdinand de Morales with a great Galeon, laden on the King's account, to Trade at Pegu. As soon as arrived at that Port, the King won him with Promises and Favours, to aid him against the King of Brama, who invaded that Country with such a Power, that the two Armies consisted of two Millions of Men and

10,000 Elephants. Morales went into a Galliot, and Commanding the Fleet of Pegu, made great havock among the Enemies Ships. Brama came on by Land like a Torrent, carrying all before him, and his Fleet covering the River, though as great as Ganges. With this Power he easily gained the City and Kingdom of Pegu. Ferdinand Morales met the Fleet with his, in respect of the other scarce visible, at the Point Ginamarreca, where was a furious, bloody and desperate Fight. But the Pegu's overpowered by the Brama's deserted Morales, who alone in his Galeot maintained himself against the Enemies, performing Wonders with vast slaughter of them, till oppressed by the Multitude he was killed. But the memory of his Bravery still lives among those People."

Another more authoritative record attributes the fall of Pegu as due largely to the desertion of Takarwutbi's chief officers.[1]

[1] Phayre, p. 94. Sousa, whose story of the fate of Morales is quoted above (vol. ii. p. 10), may be presumed to have learnt something official of his countryman's death, but he gives the following quaint account of the outbreak between Taungu and Pegu which does not synchronise with Sir Arthur Phayre's historical *résumé:* "The cause of this Revolt of Brama, who was Tributary to Pegu, was this : Above 30000 Brama's laboured in the King of Pegu's Works, this being one Condition of their Vassalage. The King used to Visit them with his Women, because they delighted to see Foreigners and notable Works, and never carried any other Company. The Labourers (what Wickedness would not they in Idleness invent, who thought so much in their Labour) resolved to rob the Queens or Concubines, and suddenly murdered the King, stripped them and fled to their Country. Dacha Rupi, Heir to the deceased, was not only deprived of Means of Revenging this Villany, but even of maintaining himself, for many of his Subjexts rebelled." He then goes on to say that the Burmese king, taking advantage

But whatever may have been the final stage of the conflict, this signal victory for the ambitious young king, who was thus transferred from a mountain fastness to an ancient throne, was in the main due to the capacity of his general Bureng Naung (Branginoco), who at once pursued Takarwutbi, the fugitive fleeing up the Irawadi to Prome, where he found an asylum with Narabadi. Having thus got rid of his rival, Tabeng again displayed his kingly qualities, and, instead of plundering the rich city and the delta generally, as a typical marauder of the time would have done, he set to work to conciliate the people and to bury the recollections of past feuds. But the presence of Takarwutbi at Prome constituted a danger, and it was determined to oust him. Meanwhile the neighbouring potentates had taken alarm; the Shan king of Ava and several chiefs combined to help Narabadi in what they felt to be a common cause; and by the time that Tabeng and his victorious general appeared before the city they were confronted by a formidable array. For some reason a battle was avoided, and Tabeng, after capturing the King of Ava's boats, retired. In vain the unfortunate Takarwutbi urged his allies to fall upon the retreating army. In his despair he followed his enemies into the delta at the head of a small band of devoted

of this opportunity, swept over the city and then the adjoining states. Dacha Rupi, no doubt, is intended for Takarwutbi, and we have already seen that he had been on the throne some thirteen years when his capital fell. Lieutenant-General Fytche, in his "Burma," adopts this story, and confuses Branginoco, the general, with Tabeng Shwehti, the king (vol. i. p. 42).

followers, and was seen no more. Thus, about 1540, disappeared the last of the line of Talaing kings founded by Wareru, *circa* 1300.

Sack of Martaban.

Having secured the first great prize in his scheme of conquest, Tabeng cast his eyes upon the flourishing Viceroyalty of Martaban. He sent a summons to Soabinya, demanding his allegiance to the new order of things at the capital, and probably if the Viceroy had acknowledged the conqueror he would have been treated with consideration. But he had a large native force at his disposal, and doubtless many fugitives had found their way to Martaban, full of resentment and not yet rid of their national contempt for the hill prince, whose audacity was to them as much a matter of wonder as of fear. Moreover, Soabinya, who had doubtless heard of the gallant part taken by the Portuguese under Morales in defence of the capital, trusted to the prowess of his European allies. He refused the summons, and Tabeng, with his able general Bureng Naung, at once advanced. The defences of Martaban were on an elaborate scale. Earthworks and a deep ditch protected the town on the land side, a number of European vessels, heavily armed and manned by Portuguese and Mussulmans, were on the sea front, and on the opposite side of the Salwin River (near the site of the present Maulmain) was a stockaded fort. The Burmese mobilised an immense army and collected a numerous fleet, enlisting at the same time a large number of mercenaries, including several hundred Portuguese, who, under the command of John Cayero (or Caeyro), do not appear to have hesitated to fight their own countrymen and their faithful commercial ally. The Commander of the Portuguese contingent in the city was Paulo de Seixas of Obidos, and he seems to have held a responsible position. The spectacle thus presented by the two bands of mercenaries, in whom each of the rival potentates reposed the utmost confidence, whilst flattering to the personal prowess of the adventurers, tells its own tale of the relations of Portugal with Burma; the men were under no sort of control from either Malacca or Goa, either at this period or at any time. The city held out for no less than seven months, despite repeated assaults, till at last famine compelled Soabinya to sue for peace and accept the conqueror's terms; these were merely that his life should be spared—a promise which was not fulfilled. The flourishing city was sacked and burnt to the ground, the unfortunate inhabitants being slaughtered in thousands. Phayre, who states that the Burmese army numbered 130,000 men, fixes the date of the siege, according to the Burmese history, at 1540–1; the Portuguese account gives the date 1544–5.

Ferdinand Mendes Pinto supplies us with some curious details in connection with the siege.[1] He

[1] Phayre, p. 265, has a good word to say for this extraordinary adventurer, whose reputation as chronicler and traveller has borne the weight of two centuries of obloquy. After quoting teh well-known sentence, "Ferdinand Mendez Pinto was but a type of thee, thou liar of the first magnitude" (Congreve's "Love for Love," act ii. scene v.), Sir Arthur remarks that "his name has become, though unjustly, a byword for untruthfulness." He points out that Pinto does not make himself a hero, nor

asserts that he arrived at Martaban as a messenger from Pedro de Faria, Governor of Malacca, to the Viceroy, with presents and letters to confirm the treaty and league of peace. Soabinya (whom he describes as the Chaubainhaa, a name, or title, adopted by Sousa), driven to desperation by his impending fate, offered Cayero, who was in command of 700 Portuguese, a great bribe to assist him and his family to escape. Seixas undertook the mission, penetrating the Burmese camp in disguise. He quite satisfied his countrymen as to the Viceroy's immense wealth, but personal jealousy appears to have prevented the plot. The spoil of the city, it seems, had been promised to the foreign leaguers, but Tabeng ordered the twenty-four gates to be strictly guarded for two days, during which the palace treasures were removed, and then by the firing of a signal gun the rapine and outrage commenced. Such was the rush of the motley crew from the Burmese camp that 300 of the soldiery were crushed to death at the city gates, and during the three days of indescribable horrors Tabeng, or his general, was obliged to enter and interfere several times to appease the mercenaries, who began to fall upon each other. By some means Seixas got out of the city with a native woman,

does he exaggerate the wealth of the kings of Indo-China, and the strength of their armies, more than other sixteenth-century travellers, and adds : "The historical events he narrates, which can be compared with the native and other accounts, are correctly told." Cogan's translation of Pinto's "Voyages and Travels" (1653, ch. 49 *et seq.*) has been utilised for these events.

whom he married at Coromandel. The unfortunate Viceroy had presented him with two valuable bracelets, assumedly in recognition of faithful service, these, says Pinto with characteristic detail, he disposed of for 36,000 ducats, the dealers afterwards selling them to a native Governor of Narsinga for 80,000 ducats.

Soabinya's fate was a sad one. Dressed in black velvet, with head and eyebrows shaven, and mounted on a small elephant, the Viceroy, who was followed by a weeping procession consisting of his wife and four small children, the ladies of his court, and several native priests, was brought out of the city through a double line of soldiers. After the sack, Tabeng promptly executed the wretched wife and children, and no less than 140 of the ladies, hanging them by the feet to gallows erected on the summit of a hill. But this villainy proved too much for even the mercenaries, and caused such a commotion in camp as to have the effect of preserving the wretched Soabinya from some nameless torture; the following night he and a number of his nobles were thrown into the sea with stones attached to their necks.

Fall of Prome. Death of Tabeng.

In celebration of his victory Tabeng, on his return, was solemnly consecrated as king, and he ordered new Htis to be placed on the two national pagodas. Prome was the next kingdom to fall into his hands. After driving the forces of the King of Ava to the very gates of the city, Tabeng fell back upon the ancient Burmese capital, Pagan, where, in pursuance of his great national enterprise, he was again declared king,

Bureng Naung now being recognised as heir-apparent. Pinto, who tells his story with sundry quaint expressions of disgust at what he witnessed, went on the expedition to Prome, having been sent a prisoner to Pegu through the treachery of one Gonzalo Falcan, a fellow-countryman, at Martaban. He again supplies a catalogue of horrors occurring during the siege and at the fall of the city. The Queen, a woman of thirty-six years, was flogged to death, her husband (and nephew), a boy of thirteen years, being tied to her body and thrown into the river. Such were the experiences of the Portuguese mercenaries in these parts, and yet there appears to have been no lack of readiness to take service on one side or the other.

After an insignificant and unsuccessful expedition against Arakan, a quarrel arose with Siam. In 1548 an immense army, including a company of about 180 Portuguese under James Soarez de Melo, marched against Odia (Ayudha), the then capital, which is described as being no less than eight leagues in circumference. Here the Burmese met with a decided check. About fifty Portuguese, commanded by James Pereira, formed part of the garrison, and the walls were mounted with many guns of unusually heavy calibre. The siege dragged on; it is stated that the invaders endeavoured to induce Pereira to desert his post but without effect, and at last they were compelled to make a disastrous retreat out of the country.[1] This signal reverse had the worst effect

[1] Phayre, who calculates that the operations lasted five months, points out that the besiegers were in the end glad to

upon Tabeng, who, although he had enjoyed a brilliant reign of eighteen years, was still only about thirty-four years of age. Giving himself up to all kinds of dissipation, he made a boon companion of a nephew of Soarez till the general, Bureng Naung, still faithful to his master, expelled the young man from the country. In this state of affairs a scion of the Talaing Royal House, Thaminhtoa, who is known in the Portuguese chronicles as Xemindoo, raised a rebellion in the city of Pegu, but it was soon crushed. The career of Tabeng Shwehti, however, was now nearing its close, and it is singular that the end was brought about by a member of the deposed race to whom, in his better days, he himself had allowed some measure of power, which had been continued. He was invited by the Governor of Sitang to witness the capture of an elephant in the jungle, when he was set upon and assassinated.[1]

Bureng Naung's empire.

The object of this somewhat lengthy review of Burmese history has been to illustrate the foundation of an empire which was near the height of its power when the first Englishman visited it, and also to afford a passing glance at the position of the Portuguese who claimed

treat with the Siamese, which they were the better able to do as they had captured the king's son-in-law. He states that the invasion was provoked by an incursion of a Siamese force in Tavoy (p. 101).

[1] The name or title of the Governor, according to Phayre (p. 102), was Thaminsoadwut. Sousa (vol. ii. p. 136) calls him the Ximi de Zatan, and adds, "Ximi is equivalent to a Duke, and he really was one of Satan's creating."

supremacy in all these seas. A very brief outline will therefore suffice of the long and prosperous reign of Bureng Naung (Branginoco), who, although he was undoubtedly the chief means of Tabeng's successes in his scheme of conquest, only completed, as king, the work of Burmese supremacy already begun.

The city of Pegu having fallen into the hands of the Governor of Sitang through the cowardice of his brother, Bureng Naung retired to Taungu to prepare for what proved to be another brilliant series of conquests. Meantime the other Talaing pretender, Thaminhtoa (Xemindoo), captured the usurper of Sitang and beheaded him, assuming royal honours in his stead. Bureng Naung lost no time in vindicating his claim to the throne. Having secured Taungu, Prome, and all the country up to Pagan, he marched on Pegu (1551) and, encountering his rival outside the walls, defeated him. Thaminhtoa fled for his life, reaching Martaban in an open boat, but eventually fell into the hands of his enemy, who treated him with contumely. Pinto, in an account of his execution, says Xemindoo was mounted on a sorry jade with the executioner riding behind him, a straw crown decorated with mussel shells was placed on his head, and he wore an iron collar trimmed with onions. Sousa adds a touch of pathos to the story: "Xemindoo fled to the Mountains, where he married a poor Fellows Daughter. He discovered himself to her, and she revealed it to her Father, at such time as great Rewards were proposed to such as should discover him. The Father-in-Law delivered him up to the King, who cut off his Head."[1] The new conqueror, having had himself consecrated "King of Kings," with his eldest son as heir-apparent, sent one of his brothers as king tributary to Martaban. His next great exploit was to rid the old Burmese throne of Ava of its Shan occupant, the city being taken by assault in 1555. It is remarkable that in this expedition, which was undertaken, ostensibly, to help the Shan king to suppress a rebel at Monyin, he is said to have had "a bodyguard of 400 Portuguese, dressed in uniform and armed with arquebuses." With characteristic pride Sousa (vol. ii. p. 237) retails another story to show the high esteem in which his fellow-countrymen were held. During the absence of the King of Kings a rebellion broke out in Pegu city, and the Queen was obliged to fly to the castle, where she was protected by thirty-nine Portuguese. On his return, Bureng Naung sent for the men who defended the Queen, and the officer "brought him some Moors of Note; but the King, knowing the Portuguese were the men, said in Anger, 'I sent you for Men, and you bring me Cowards; Go bring me Men.'" The Portuguese were then rewarded "with riches, Praises, and Honour."

With the exception of a campaign in Zimmé (1558), which resulted in that country being placed under tribute, the whole empire remained at peace till 1562. In the meantime Bureng Naung had

[1] Vol. ii. p. 137. Phayre (p. 105) states that Thaminhtoa, or Xemindoo ("Shemindoo," as Fitch calls him), is recognised in the Talaing chronicles as Zaggali Meng; he was the last reigning Peguan Prince.

beautified his capital so that it became the admiration of all European visitors. He prohibited certain barbarous rites among the Shans, forbade his own people to worship Nats or familiars, and endeavoured generally to re-establish a higher form of Buddhism throughout the country. Cæsar Frederick, who visited the capital a few years later (1569), gives an enthusiastic description of the sovereign's power and magnificence. He states, "This king of Pegu hath not any army or power by sea, but in the land, for people, dominions, golde and silver, he farre exceeds the power of the great Turke in treasure and strength." It was, however, his great desire to acquire one of the four sacred white elephants in possession of the King of Siam which led him, in spite of the disastrous experience of the previous reign, to launch an expedition against that kingdom in 1563. A huge force swept down the valley of the Menam in four divisions, and by March, 1564, the capital had fallen, Bramahin, son of the deposed potentate, being placed on the throne as tributary king. Another expedition against Zimmé followed in the same year, but during Bureng Naung's absence two rebellious outbreaks occurred in the city of Pegu, the second and more serious one being led by a Shan captive. The King of Kings, who had by this time again subdued Zimmé, returned and was so enraged against the Peguan rebels that he ordered al the prisoners and their families to be placed in a huge wicker-work building and burnt to death. But, so far as one can judge from the records of his reign Bureng Naung, personally, had no predilection for torture and outrage, and in this instance he eventually forgave all the rebels but their leaders.

Last Conquest. Death of Branginoco. Another period of peace followed, and was only broken as the result of Bureng Naung's magnanimity. The ex-king of Siam, having become a devotee, was allowed to return home to worship, taking with him the widow and children of his younger son. Bramahin, finding that the conqueror now held no hostages, threw off the suzerainty, with the result that in 1568 another great Burmese force came down upon Odia (Ayudha) and invested it. After a siege of four months the city again fell, and this time was sacked. One account states that the victory was won by a trick. A Siamese noble of high rank, who was in the invading army, pretended to desert and appeared before Bramahin with chains on his legs. He was warmly received and given an important command, which he, of course, betrayed. The King of Kings returned to Pegu after this, his final, conquest in 1570. The empire, which extended from the Shan hill country in the north to the capital of Siam in the south-east, was at peace, with the exception of insignificant enterprises, for the next ten years, for Bureng Naung now occupied an impregnable position. There was only one country left unconquered which had formerly acknowledged Burmese sway. This was Arakan, which lay beyond the western hills, and to complete the task begun by Tabeng he determined (1579) to subdue it, commencing operations by despatching a formidable fleet. On the way to the western coast the Burmese force beat off several

Portuguese vessels which tried to bar its progress, and the invaders landed at Sandoway in readiness for Bureng Naung's arrival. But, after waiting more than a year, the expedition so auspiciously begun was suddenly interrupted by the news of the king's death, in November, 1581.

Thus ended the thirty years' reign of Bureng Naung (Branginoco), who died at the zenith of his glory, and whose capital city of Pegu had become one of the greatest centres of wealth and commerce in the Further East. His characteristics, exhibited throughout a career which began in the obscure Taungu valley and reached its object, the throne of an empire, have been but faintly indicated in this necessarily condensed account of a phase of Eastern history which is not well known even in our own time. As to its romance and astonishing results, we may find some parallel to the story of Bureng Naung in that of Alaunghpra (Alompra), with whom we Britishers came into contact at a later period; but for the solid qualities of the conquering and administrative ruler Bureng Naung stands alone in the Burmese annals. With regard to the mysterious Portuguese strangers, he succeeded in a line of policy which, so far as he could comprehend it, was the best for his country. He welcomed them as general and sovereign, but it was only to make use of them, and to him they were hirelings—nothing more.

CHAPTER II

NARRATIVE CONTINUED—THE FIRST ENGLISHMAN IN PEGU (BURMA)—HIS PREDECESSORS—THE "VERY GREAT, STRONG AND VERY FAIRE" CITY

IN continuing his adventurous journey still further east, Master Ralph Fitch won for himself the title of the first Englishman in Burma—an honour which we in these days are better able to appreciate than were his contemporaries. Sailing from the Sunderbunds down the coast of Arakan, he tells us he crossed the bar of Negrais and, visiting several places in the Irawadi delta *en route*, he appears to have spent some time in the city both in 1587 and on his return from Malacca in 1588. At this time Nanda Bureng, who succeeded his father, the powerful Branginoco, in 1581, was on the throne, and, according to the records, had just commenced the series of ill-directed attempts upon Siam which led to the ruin of the glorious capital described by Fitch, the eventual devastation of the whole surrounding region and his own captivity and death at Taungu in 1599, after a reign of eighteen years. The early

European predecessors of the British traveller who left any record of their impressions of Burma or Pegu are but few in number. They come in the following order as to date, namely, Marco Polo, at the end of the thirteenth century; Nicolo di Conti, a Venetian, at the beginning of the fifteenth; Athanasius Nikitin of Twer, a Russian, 1468–74; Hieronimo di Santo Stefano, a Genoese, 1496; Lewes Vertomannus (Varthema), of Rome, who speaks of Armenians and Nestorians as being in Pegu, 1503–4. After the opening up of the Cape route and the trafficking with the Portuguese, referred to in the preceding chapter, comes Cæsar Frederick, the Venetian, about 1567–9, whose account of the great city as he saw it in Branginoco's days (preserved by both Hakluyt and Purchas) is full of interest. Fitch's immediate predecessor was Gasparo Balbi, a Venetian jeweller, who arrived in 1583, and who has also left a graphic record. As to the ruin of the country soon after the return of our traveller, Nicolas Pimenta, a Portuguese priest who came in 1598, gives some account.[1]

[1] For the various references see Phayre, chap. xxii.; Major's "India in the Fifteenth Century" (Hakluyt Society) for Conti and Nikitin; "The Travels of Ludovico di Varthema," by Mr. Winter Jones and the Rev. G. Percy Badger (Hakluyt Society). Balbi states that he left Aleppo in December, 1579, and, following the usual route to Goa, continued his journey *viâ* Cochin, Cananor, Ceylon, Negapatan, and St. Thomas. He crossed the bar of Negrais in September, 1583, and gives an interesting account of his voyage through the delta and a description of the capital (Purchas, 1625, vol. ii. book x., which also contains the narrative of Pimenta).

The modern town of Pegu, which lies close to the bank of the river of the same name, is forty-six miles north-east of Rangoon. It occupies portion of the site of the old city, and in 1881 had a population of only 5,891. In his " Embassy to Ava " Symes states that the extent of ancient Pegu could be accurately traced by the ditch and wall: " from these it appears to have been a quadrangle, each side measuring nearly a mile and a half." He estimated the breadth of the ditch at 60 yards, and the depth 10 or 12 feet; the height of the wall he conjectured at 30 feet at least, and the breadth at the base not less than 40 feet; it was built of brick with bastions about 300 yards apart, and a parapet of masonry. The Great Pagoda, founded according to tradition more than two thousand years ago, is still a conspicuous object, and according to Hunter, the Shwe-maw-daw at Pegu is held in greater veneration by the Talaings than the Shwe-Dagon at Rangoon. Symes writes of it: " This extraordinary pile of buildings is erected on a double terrace, one raised upon another; the lower and greater terrace is about 10 feet above the natural level of the ground, forming an exact parallelogram; the upper and lesser terrace is similar in shape, and rises about 20 feet above the lower terrace, or 30 above the level of the country. I judged a side of the lower terrace to be 1,391 feet; of the upper, 684." The temple he describes as of brick and mortar, octagonal at the base and spiral at the top, each side of the base measuring 162 feet. Fifty-seven small spires are placed on a ledge near the base, and fifty-three more on a higher ledge.

THE GREAT SCHWE-MAW-DAW PAGODA, PEGU.

The whole is surmounted by a gilt "tee" (hti), or umbrella, which is to be seen on every sacred building, and the extreme height of the edifice from the ground is 361 feet. The title "Shoemadoo," or Golden Supreme, he suggests comes from "Shoe," or "Shœ," golden, and "Madoo," a corruption of "Mahadeva," or deo.[1] It is scarcely necessary to add that the present centre of government and national life on this coast is the flourishing modern city of Rangoon, which was also founded by a native conqueror under circumstances not less stirring than those recorded in the preceding pages. Master Fitch's journal of this portion of his travels is full of life and movement, and panoramic in its minuteness.

BURMA—THE JOURNEY (THIRD PART).

"I went from Serrepore the 28. of Nouember 1586. for Pegu in a small ship or foist of one Albert Carauallos, and so passing downe Ganges, and passing by the Island of Sundiua, porto Grande, or the countrie of Tippera, the kingdom of Recon and Mogen, leauing them on our left side with a faire wind at Northwest: our course was South & by East, which brought vs to the barre of Negrais in Pegu: if any contrary wind had come, we had throwen many of our things ouer-boord: for we were

Sundiua Island.

[1] "Embassy to Ava," by Lieut.-Col. Symes (1800). The mission took place in 1795.

so pestered with people & goods, that there was scant place to lie in. From Bengala to Pegu is 90. leagues. We entred the barre of Negrais, which is a braue barre & hath 4. fadomes of water where it hath least. Three dayes after we came to Cosmin, which is a very pretie towne, and standeth very pleasantly, very well furnished with all things.[1] The people be very tall & well disposed ; the women white, round faced, with little eies : the houses are high built, set vpon great high postes, & they go vp to them with long ladders for feare of the Tygers which be very many. The countrey is very fruitful of all things. Here are very great Figs, Orenges, Cocoes, and other fruits. The land is very high that we fall withall, but after we be entred the barre, it is very lowe and full of riuers, for they goe all too and fro in boates, which they call paroes, and keepe their houses with wife and children in them.

Negrais.

Cosmin.

Ladders vsed to auoyd the danger of wild beasts.

Dwelling in boats.

"From the barre of Nigrais to the

[1] Cosmin, a corruption of Kusimanagara, now the important town and port of Bassein, Burma, situated on both banks of the Bassein river in the Irawadi delta, seventy-five miles from the sea. It is said to have been founded by a Talaing or Peguan princess in 1249. It is difficult, if not impossible, to identify all the places Fitch mentions in the delta. The changes in the district have been great ; as Hunter puts it, he and other travellers "found Rangoon a village."

citie of Pegu is ten dayes iourney by the riuers. Wee went from Cosmin to Pegu in Paroes or boates, and passing

Medon.

vp the riuers wee came to Medon, which is a prety towne, where there be a wonderfull number of Paroes, for they keepe their houses and their markets in them all vpon the water. They rowe too and fro, and haue all their marchandizes in their boates with a great Sombrero or shadow ouer their heads to keepe the sunne from them, which is as broad as a great cart wheele made of the leaues of the Coco trees and fig trees, and is very light.

Dela.

"From Medon we went to Dela, which is a very faire towne, and hath a faire port into the sea, from whence go many ships to Malacca, Mecca, and many other places. Here are 18. or 20. very great and long houses, where they tame and keep many elephants of the kings: for there about in the wildernesse they catch the wilde elephants. It is a very fruitfull countrey. From Dela we

Cirion.

went to Cirion, which is a good towne, and hath a faire porte into the sea, whither come many ships from Mecca, Malacca, Sumatra, and from diuers other places.[1] And there the ships staie

[1] Cirion, Syriam, or Than-Lyin, on the left bank of the Pegu river and about three miles from its mouth (H.). This was the

and discharge, & send vp their goods in Paroes to Pegu. From Cirion we went to Macao,[1] which is a pretie towne, where we left our boats or Paroes, & in the morning taking Delingeges, which are a kind of Coches made of cords & cloth quilted, & caried vpon a stang[2] betweene 3. or 4. men : we came to Pegu the same day.[3]

Macao.

Coches carried on mens shoulders.

Pegu.

"Pegu is a citie very great, strong, and very faire, with walles of stone, and great ditches round about it. There are two townes, the old towne and the newe. In the old towne are all the marchants strangers, and very many marchants of the countrey. All the goods are sold in the olde towne which is very great, and hath many suburbes round about it, and all the houses are made of Canes which they call Bambos

scene of the exploits of Philip de Brito, a Portuguese adventurer, who for a time dominated the whole delta.

[1] Meh-Kay (?). [2] Or pole.

[3] Referring to the journey through the delta, Lieut.-General Fytche in his "Burma," vol. i. p. 11, makes the following interesting comment : "Singular enough, I traversed myself probably the very same route through these creeks while in pursuit of some marauding bands, during the second Burmese war, and was the second Englishman that had done so. At least, there is no record of any other having gone this route during the interval. The passage had become much blocked up from disuse and the banks overgrown with trees, which had to be cleared in many parts before the gunboats could pass through."

and bee couered with strawe. In your house you haue a Warehouse which they call Godon,[1] which is made of bricke to put your goods in, for oftentimes they take fire and burne in an houre foure or fiue hundred houses: so that if the Godon were not, you should bee in danger to haue all burned, if any winde should rise, at a trice. In the newe towne is the king, and all his Nobilitie and Gentrie. It is a citie very great and populous, and is made square and with very faire walles, and a great ditch round about it full of water, with many crocodiles in it: it hath twenty gates, and they bee made of stone, for euery square fiue gates. There are also many Turrets for Centinels to watch, made of wood, and gilded with golde very faire. The streets are the fairest that euer I saw, as straight as a line from one gate to the other, and so broad that tenne or twelue men may ride a front thorow them. On both sides of them at euery mans doore is set a palmer tree which is the nut tree, which make a very faire shew and a very commodious shadow, so that a man may walke in the shade all day. The houses be made of wood, and couered with tiles. The kings house is in the middle of the city, and

[1] Or godown.

is walled and ditched round about: and the buildings within are made of wood very sumptuously gilded, and great workemanship is vpon the forefront, which is likewise very costly gilded. And the house wherein his Pagode or idole standeth is couered with tiles of siluer, and all the walles are gilded with golde. Within the first gate of the kings house is a great large roome, on both sides whereof are houses made for the kings elephants, which be maruellous great and faire, and are brought up to warres and in seruice of the king. And among the rest he hath foure white elephants, which are very strange and rare: for there is none other king which hath them but he: if any other king hath one, hee will send vnto him for it. When any of these white elephants is brought vnto the king, all the merchants in the city are commanded to see them, and to giue him a present of halfe a ducat, which doth come to a great summe: for that there are many merchants in the city. After that you haue giuen your present you may come and see them at your pleasure, although they stand in the kings house. This king in his title is called the king of the white elephants. If any other king haue one, and will

Foure white elephants.

The king of the white elephants.

not send it him, he will make warre with him for it: for he had rather lose a great part of his kingdome, then not to conquere him. They do very great seruice vnto these white elephants; euery one of them standeth in an house gilded with golde, and they doe feede in vessels of siluer and gilt. One of them when he doth go to the riuer to be washed, as euery day they do, goeth vnder a canopy of cloth of golde or of silke carried ouer him by sixe or eight men, and eight or ten men goe before him playing on drummes, shawmes, or other instruments: and when he is washed and commeth out of the riuer, there is a gentleman which doth wash his feet in a siluer basin: which is his office giuen him by the king. There is no such account made of any blacke elephant, be he neuer so great. And surely there be woonderfull faire and great, and some be nine cubites in height. And they do report that the king hath aboue fiue thousand elephants of warre, besides many other which be not taught to fight.

"This king hath a very large place wherein he taketh the wilde elephants. It standeth about a mile from Pegu, builded with a faire court within, and is in a great groue or wood: and there be many huntsmen, which go into the wildernesse with the elephants: for without the she they are not to be taken. And they be taught for that purpose: and euery hunter hath fiue or sixe of them: and they say that they anoint the she elephants with a certaine ointment, which when the wild elephant doth smell, he will not leaue her. When they haue brought the wilde elephant neere vnto the place, they send word vnto the towne, and many horsemen and footmen come out and cause the she elephant to enter into a strait way which doeth go to the palace, and the she and he do runne in: for it is like a wood: and when they be in, the gate doth shut. Afterward they get out the female: and when the male seeth that he is left alone, he weepeth and crieth, and runneth against the walles, which be made of so strong trees, that some of them doe break their teeth with running against them. Then they pricke him with sharpe canes, & cause him to go into a strait house, and there they put a rope about his middle and about his feet, and let him stand there three or foure dayes without eating or drinking: and then they bring a female to him, with meat and drinke, and within few dayes he becommeth tame.

The chiefe force of the king is in these elephants. And when they go into the warres they set a frame of wood vpon their backes, bound with great cordes, within sit foure or sixe men, which fight with gunnes, bowes and arrowes, darts and other weapons. And they say that their skinnes are so thicke that a pellet of an harquebush will scarce pearce them, except it be in some tender place. Their weapons be very badde. They haue gunnes, but shoot very badly in them, darts and swordes short without points.

"The king keepeth a very great state: when he sitteth abroad as he doth euery day twise, all his noble men which they call Shemines sit on ech side, a good distance off, and a great guard without them. The Court yard is very great. If any man will speake with the king, he is to kneele downe, to heaue vp his hands to his head, and to put his head to the ground three times, when he entreth, in the middle way, and when he commeth neere to the king: and then he sitteth downe and talketh with the king: if the king like well of him, he sitteth neere him within three or foure paces: if he thinke not well of him, he sitteth further off. When he goeth to warre, he goeth very strong. At my

Odia a city in Siam.

being there he went to Odia in the countrey of Siam with three hundred thousand men, and fiue thousand elephants. Thirty thousand men were his guard. These people do eate roots, herbs, leaues, dogs, cats, rats, serpents, and snakes; they refuse almost nothing. When the king rideth abroad, he rideth with a great guard, and many noblemen, oftentimes vpon an elephant with a fine castle vpon him very fairly gilded with gold; and sometimes vpon a great frame like an horsliter, which hath a little house vpon it couered ouer head, but open on the sides, which is all gilded with golde, & set with many rubies and saphires, whereof he hath infinite store in his country, and is caried vpon sixteene or eighteene mens shoulders. This coach in their language is called Serrion. Very great feasting and triumphing is many times before the king both of men and women. This king hath little force by Sea, because hee hath but very few ships. He hath houses full of golde and siluer, and bringeth in often, but spendeth very little, and hath the mines of rubies and saphires, and spinelles.

This maner of cariage on mens shoulders is vsed in Peru, and in Florida.

"Neere vnto the palace of the king, there is a treasure woonderfull rich; the which because it is so neere, he doth not account of it: and it standeth open for all men to see in a great walled court with two gates, which be alwayes open. There are foure houses gilded very richly, and couered with leade: in euery one of them are Pagodes or images of huge stature and great value. In the first is the picture of a king in golde with a crowne of golde on his head full of great rubies and saphires, and about him there stand foure children of golde. In the second house is the picture of a man in siluer woonderfull great, as high as an house; his foot is as long as a man, and he is made sitting, with a crowne on his head very rich with stones. In the third house is the picture of a man greater then the other, made of brasse, with a rich crowne on his head. In the fourth and last house doth stand another, made of brasse greater then the other, with a crowne also on his head very rich with stones. In another court not farre from this stand foure other Pagodes or idoles, maruellous great, of copper, made in the same place where they do stand; for they be so great that they be not to be remooued: they stand in foure houses gilded very faire, and are themselues gilded all ouer saue their heads, and they shew like a blacke Morian. Their expences in gilding of their images are wonderfull.[1] The king hath one wife and aboue three hundred concubines, by which they say he hath fourescore or fourescore and ten children. He sitteth in iudgment almost euery day. They vse no speech, but giue vp their supplications written in the leaues of a tree with the point of an yron bigger then a bodkin. These leaues are an elle long, and about two inches broad; they are also double. He which giueth in his supplication, doth stand in a place a little distance off with a present. If his matter be liked of, the king accepteth of his present, and granteth his request: if his sute be not liked of, he returneth with his present; for the king will not take it.

Paper of the leaues of a tree.

"In India there are few commodities which serue for Pegu, except Opium of Cambaia, painted cloth of S. Thome, or of Masulipatan, and white cloth of Bengala, which is spent there in great quantity. They bring thither also much cotton yarne red coloured with a root which they call Saia, which will neuer lose his colour: it is very wel solde here, and very much of it commeth yerely to Pegu. By your mony you lose much. The ships which come from Bengala, S. Thome, and Masulipatan,

An excellent colour with a root called Saia.

[1] Possibly Fitch refers to the national Pagoda at Pegu.

come to the bar of Nigrais and to Cosmin. To Martauan a port of the sea in the kingdome of Pegu come many ships from Malacca laden with Sandall, Porcelanes? and other wares of China, and with Camphora of Borneo, and Pepper from Achen in Sumatra. To Cirion a port of Pegu come ships from Mecca with woollen cloth, Scarlets, Veluets, Opium, and such like. There are in Pegu eight Brokers, whom they call Tareghe, which are bound to sell your goods at the price which they be woorth, and you giue them for their labour two in the hundred: and they be bound to make your debt good, because you sell your marchandises vpon their word. If the Broker pay you not at his day, you may take him home, and keepe him in your house: which is a great shame for him. And if he pay you not presently, you may take his wife and children and his slaues, and binde them at your doore, and set them in the Sunne; for that is the law of the countrey. Their current money in these parts is a kinde of brasse which they call Gansa, wherewith you may buy golde, siluer, rubies, muske, and all other things. The golde and siluer is marchandise, and is worth sometimes more, and sometimes lesse, as other wares

Woollen cloth and scarlets solde in Pegu.

The money of Pegu.

be. This brasen money doeth goe by a weight which they call a biza; and commonly this biza after our account is worth about halfe a crowne or somewhat lesse. The marchandise which be in Pegu, are golde, siluer, rubies, saphires, spinelles, muske, beniamim or franck-incense, long pepper, tinne, leade, copper, lacca whereof they make hard ware, rice, and wine made of rice, and some sugar. The elephants doe eate the sugar canes, or els they would make very much. And they consume many canes likewise in making of their Varellaes or Idole temples, which are in great number both great and small. They be made round like a sugar loafe, some are as high as a Church, very broad beneath, some a quarter of a mile in compasse: within they be all earth done about with stone. They consume in these Varellaes great quantity of golde; for that they be all gilded aloft: and many of them from the top to the bottome: and euery ten or twelue yeeres they must be new gilded, because the rain consumeth off the golde: for they stand open abroad. If they did not consume their golde in these vanities, it would be very plentifull and good cheape in Pegu.

The seuerall merchandises of Pegu.

The forme of their Temples or Varellaes.

"About two dayes iourney from

Pegu there is a Varelle or Pagode, which is the pilgrimage of the Pegues: it is called Dogonne, and is of a woonderfull bignesse, and all gilded from the foot to the toppe.[1] And there is an house by it wherein the Tallipoies which are their Priests doe preach. This house is fiue and fifty paces in length, and hath three pawnes or walks in it, and forty great pillars gilded, which stand betweene the walks; and it is open on all sides with a number of small pillars, which be likewise gilded: it is gilded with golde within and without. There are houses very faire round about for the pilgrims to lie in: and many goodly houses for the Tallipoies to preach in, which are full of images both of men and women, which are all gilded ouer with golde. It is the fairest place, as I suppose, that is in the world: it standeth very high, and there are foure wayes to it, which all along are set with trees of fruits, in such wise that a man man goe in the shade aboue two miles in length. And when their feast day is, a man can hardly passe by water or by land for the great presse of people; for they come from all places of the kingdome of Pegu thither at their feast.

The Tallipoies or Priests of Pegu.

[1] The great Shwe-Dagon Pagoda at Rangoon.

"In Pegu they haue many Tallipoies or priests, which preach against all abuses. Many men resort vnto them. When they enter into their kiack, that is to say, their holy place or temple, at the doore there is a great iarre of water with a cocke or a ladle in it, and there they wash their feet; and then they enter in, and lift vp their hands to their heads first to their preacher, and then to the Sunne, and so sit downe. The Tallipoies go very strangely apparelled with one camboline or thinne cloth next to their body of a browne colour, another of yellow doubled many times vpon their shoulder: and those two be girded to them with a broad girdle: and they haue a skinne of leather hanging on a string about their necks, whereupon they sit, bare headed & bare footed; for none of them weareth shooes; with their right armes bare and a great broad sombrero or shadow in their hands to defend them in the Summer from the Sunne, and in the Winter from the raine. When the Tallipoies or priests take their Orders, first they go to schoole vntill they be twenty yeres olde or more, and then they come before a Tallipoie appointed for that purpose, whom they call Rowli: he is of the chiefest and most learned, and

The apparell their priests.

he opposeth them, and afterward examineth them many times, whether they will leaue their friends, and the company of all women, and take vpon them the habit of a Tallipoie. If any be content, then he rideth vpon an horse about the streets very richly apparelled, with drummes and pipes, to shew that he leaueth the riches of the world to be a Tallipoie. In few daies after, he is caried vpon a thing like an horstliter, which they call a serion, vpon ten or twelue mens shoulders in the apparell of a Tallipoie, with pipes and drummes, and many Tallipoies with him, and al his friends, and so they go with him to his house, which standeth without the towne, and there they leaue him. Euery one of them hath his house, which is very little, set vpon six or eight posts, and they go vp to them with a ladder of twelue or foureteene staues. Their houses be for the most part by the hie wayes side, and among the trees, and in the woods. And they go with a great pot made of wood or fine earth, and couered, tied with a broad girdle vpon their shoulder, which commeth vnder their arme, wherewith they go to begge their victuals which they eate, which is rice, fish, and herbs. They demand nothing, but come to the doore, and the people presently doe giue them, some one thing and some another: and they put all together in their potte: for they say they must eate of their almes, and therewith content themselues. They keepe their feasts by the Moone: and when it is new Moone they keepe their greatest feast: and then the people send rice and other things to that kiack or church of which they be; and there all the Tallipoies doe meete which be of that Church, and eate the victuals which are sent them. When the Tallipoies do preach, many of the people cary them gifts into the pulpit where they sit and preach. And there is one which sitteth by them to take that which the people bring. It is diuided among them. They haue none other ceremonies nor seruice that I could see, but onely preaching.

Obseruation of new moones.

Iamahey fiue & twenty dayes iourney North-eastward from Pegu.

"I went from Pegu to Iamahey, which is in the countrey of the Langeiannes, whom we call Iangomes; it is fiue and twenty dayes iourney north-east from Pegu.[1] In which iourney I passed many fruitfull and pleasant countreys. The countrey is very lowe, and hath many faire riuers. The houses are very bad, made of canes, and couered with straw. Heere are many wilde

[1] Zimmé in the Siamese Shan states.

buffes and elephants. Iamahey is a very faire and great towne, with faire houses of stone, well peopled, the streets are very large, the men very well set and strong, with a cloth about them, bare headed and bare footed: for in all these countreys they weare no shooes. The women be much fairer then those of Pegu. Heere in all these countreys they haue no wheat. They make some cakes of rice. Hither to Iamahey come many marchants out of China, and bring great store of muske, golde, siluer, and many other things of China worke. Here is great store of victuals: they haue such plenty that they will not milke the buffles, as they doe in all other places. Here is great store of copper and beniamin. In these countreys when the people be sicke they make a vow to offer meat vnto the diuell, if they escape: and when they be recouered they make a banket with many pipes & drummes and other instruments, and dansing all the night and their friends come and bring gifts, cocos, figges, arracaes, and other fruits, and with great dauncing and reioycing they offer to the diuell, and say, they giue the diuel to eat, and driue him out. When they be dancing and playing they will cry & hallow very loud; and in this sort they say they driue him away. And when they be sicke a Tallipoy or two euery night doth sit by them & sing, to please the diuell that he should not hurt them. And if any die he is caried vpon a great frame made like a tower, with a couering all gilded with golde made of canes caried with foureteene or sixteene men, with drummes and pipes and other instruments playing before him to a place out of the towne and there is burned. He is accompanied with all his friends and neighbours, all men : and they giue to the tallipoies or priests many mats and cloth : and then they returne to the house and there make a feast for two dayes : and then the wife with all the neighbours wiues & her friends go to the place where he was burned, and there they sit a certaine time add cry and gather the pieces of bones which be left unburned and bury them, and then returne to their houses and make an end of all mourning. And the men and women which be neere of kin do shaue their heads, which they do not vse except it be for the death of a friend : for they much esteeme their haire.

They burne their dead.

"Caplan is the place where they finde the rubies, saphires, and spinelles : it standeth sixe dayes iourney from Aua

Caplan is the place where the rubies and other precious stones are found.

in the kingdome of Pegu. There are many great high hilles out of which they digge them. None may go to the pits but onely those which digge them.[1] . . . . . .

"The Bramas which be of the kings countrey (for the king is a Brama) haue their legs or bellies, or some part of their body, as they thinke good themselues, made black with certaine things which they haue: they vse to pricke the skinne, and to put on it a kinde of anile or blacking, which doth continue alwayes. And this is counted an honour among them: but none may haue it but the Bramas which are of the kings kindred.[2]

The people of Pegu weare no beards.

These people weare no beards: they pull out the haire on their faces with little pinsons made for the purpose. Some of them will let 16 or 20 haires grow together, some in one place of his face and some in another, and pulleth out all the rest: for he carieth his pinsons alwayes with him to pull the haires out as soone as they appeare. If they see a man with a beard they wonder at him. They haue their teeth blacked both men and women, for they

[1] The ruby mines of the Mogok district are now worked by a British company under a concession from the Government.

[2] The practice of tattooing the upper half of the leg is still in vogue among the male population of Burma.

say a dogge hath his teeth white, therefore they will blacke theirs.

"The Pegues if they haue a sute in the law which is so doubtfull that they cannot well determine it, put two long canes into the water where it is very deepe: and both the parties go into the water by the poles, and there sit men to iudge, and they both do diue vnder the water, and he which remaineth longest vnder the water doth winne the sute."

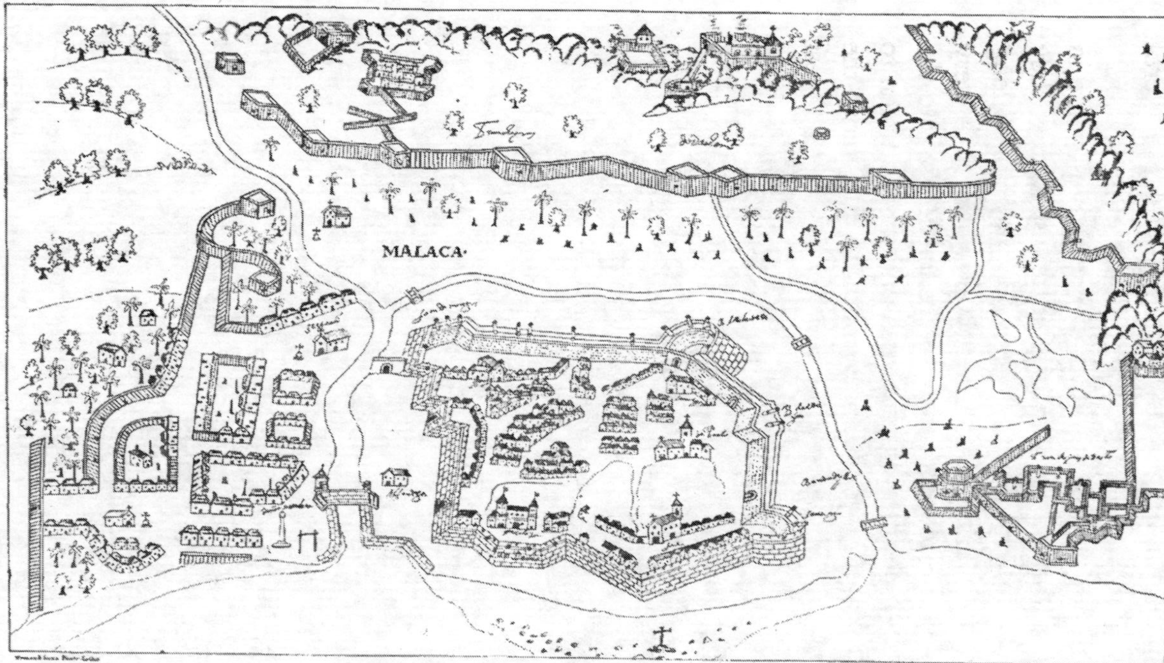

PLAN OF THE PORTUGUESE FORTRESS OF MALACA.

[British Museum, Sloane MS. 197, folio 382.]

CHAPTER III

NARRATIVE CONCLUDED—MALACCA, THE EMPORIUM—TRADE WITH CHINA AND JAPAN—CHINESE SUSPICIONS—THE RETURN

THE story of the last stages of Master Fitch's wanderings presents two notable features, namely, the ease of the traveller's movements in remote and turbulent regions, secondly, his immunity from the caprices of the native tyrant, or the jealousy and rapacity of the official or filibustering Portuguese. He travelled as a trader and paid his dues as a matter of course at the various ports he visited ; indeed he had no other means of support, for there is not the slightest suggestion that he took either part or interest in any of the plundering expeditions he must have seen going on around him.

Malacca, just before the first Englishman saw it, had undergone a terrible experience. Linschoten states that early in 1587 news reached Goa that the emporium was in great danger, the kings of Achem (Acheen) and Jor (Johore) having closed the Straits, thus blocking the spice trade and preventing traffic to China and Japan. The news caused a great sensation, and in September Dom Paulo de Lima Pereira was despatched thither with a strong force. Dom Paulo carried out the expedition with distinguished success, crushing all opposition, and, after relieving the city, which was on the verge of starvation, returned to Goa in April, 1588. The Dutch narrator, in his usual entertaining fashion, tells us that the Dom captured in the straits a ship belonging to the King of Achem, who was the principal cause of the disturbance, in which was his daughter on her way to be married to the King of Jor, who carried with her a large piece of ordnance as a wedding present. The Portuguese landed and, after a desperate resistance, plundered and burnt the capital of Jor, afterwards proceeding to Malacca, which they entered in triumph, the King of Achem being glad to come to terms for his daughter's sake. The great gun was sent as a trophy to the King of Portugal, but sunk in the wreck of the vessel off Tercera in the Azores; it was afterwards raised and placed on the fortifications of that island. Apparently the ship in question was that which Linschoten met at St. Helena on his own return home (1589).[1] On board of her he tells us was a factor "Gerrit van Afhuysen borne in Antwarpe, and dwelling in Lisbone," who had sailed in the vessel from Lisbon two years before. Fitch, who reached the city immediately after its relief by Dom Paulo, was there at the

[1] Linschoten's "Discours," English ed., 1598, pp. 151–4 and 172. Sousa gives a graphic account of the relief of Malacca and the rivalry of the Portuguese commanders, vol. iii. chap. v.; also see Danvers, vol. ii. chap. iii.

same time as the Dutchman, but the presence of the Englishman was evidently unnoticed, otherwise Afhuysen would have mentioned the circumstance to Linschoten, who with equal certainty would have left us the gossip in full detail.

After being captured by the Dutch in 1641, and by the British in 1795, the city was again held by the former from 1818 to 1825, when it finally became a British possession. Owing to the shallowness of the harbour, among other causes, the port has long been outrivalled by both Singapore and Penang. A recent traveller thus tersely describes its present condition: "Malacca is reposing after its varied history and its former prosperity as the outlet of the products of the Peninsula, in a condition of peaceful stagnation. Its colourless condition is well typified by its sole product—tapioca, produced in large quantities by Chinese labour and capital." He recalls that Camoens was wrecked off this coast on his voyage home and swam ashore with the manuscript of the Lusiad, losing everything else. The poet wrote of its prosperous days:—

> "Malacca's market grand and opulent,
> Whither each Province of the long seaboard
> Shall send of merchantry rich varied hoard."[1]

THE JOURNEY (FOURTH PART).

"The 10 of Ianuary I went from Pegu to Malacca, passing by many of

Malacca.

[1] "The Peoples and Politics of the Far East," by Mr. Henry Norman, p. 44 (Fisher Unwin, 1895).

13

the ports of Pegu, as Martauan, the Iland of Taui, from whence commeth great store of tinne which serueth all India, the Ilands of Tanaseri, Iunsalaon, and many others: and so came to Malacca the 8 of February, where the Portugals haue a castle which standeth nere the sea.[1] And the countrey fast without the towne belongeth to the Malayos, which is a kinde of proud people. They go naked with a cloth about their middle, and a litle roll of cloth about their heads. Hither come many ships from China & from the Malucos, Banda, Timor, and from many other Ilands of the Iauas, which bring great store of spices and drugs, and diamants and other iewels. The voyages into many of these Ilands belong vnto the captaine of Malacca; so that none may goe thither without his licence: which yeeld him great summes of money euery yeere. The Portugals heere haue often times warres with the king of Achem which standeth in the Iland of Sumatra: from whence commeth great store of pepper and other spices euery

[1] The chief export of the island of Tavoy during recent years has consisted of edible birds'-nests. The old town of Tenasserim was built on a neck of land at the confluence of the Great and Little Tenasserim rivers; it is now a mere hamlet (H.). Island of Junkseylon.

yeere to Pegu and Mecca within the Red sea, and other places.

The voyage to Iapan.

"When the Portugals go from Macao in China to Iapan, they carry much white silke, golde, muske, and porcelanes: and they bring from thence nothing but siluer. They haue a great caracke which goeth thither euery yere, and she bringeth from thence euery yere aboue sixe hundred thousand crusadoes: and all this siluer of Iapan, and two hundred thousand crusadoes more in siluer which they bring yeerely out of India, they imploy to their great aduantage in China: and they bring from thence golde, muske, silke, copper, porcelanes, and many other things very costly and gilded. When the Portugals come to Canton in China to traffike, they must remaine there but certaine dayes: and when they come in at the gate of the city, they must enter their names in a booke, and when they goe out at night they must put out their names. They may not lie in the towne all night, but must lie in their boats without the towne. And their dayes being expired, if any man remaine there, they are euill vsed and imprisoned. The Chinians are very suspitious, and doe not trust strangers. It is thought that the king doth not know that any strangers come

Eight hundred thousand crusadoes in siluer imployed yerely by the Portugals in China.

into his countrey. And further it is credibly reported that the common people see their king very seldome or not at all, nor may not looke vp to that place where he sitteth. And when he rideth abroad he is caried vpon a great chaire or serrion gilded very faire, wherein there is made a little house with a latise to looke out at ; so that he may see them, but they may not looke vp at him : and all the time that he passeth by them, they heaue vp their hands to their heads, & lay their heads on the ground, and looke not vp vntill he be passed. The order of China is when they mourne, that they weare white thread shoes, and hats of straw. The man doth mourne for his wife two yeeres, the wife for her husband three yeeres : the sonne for his father a yeere, and for his mother two yeres. And all the time which they mourne they keepe the dead in the house, the bowels being taken out and filled with chownam or lime, and coffined : and when the time is expired they carry them out playing and piping, and burne them. And when they returne they pull off their mourning weeds, and marry at their pleasure. A man may keepe as many concubines as he will, but one wife onely. All the Chineans, Iaponians,

The writing of the people of China, &c. and Cauchin Chineans do write right downwards, and they do write with a fine pensill made of dogs or cats haire.

Laban. "Laban is an Iland among the Iauas **Diamants.** from whence come the diamants of the New water. And they finde them in the riuers: for the king will not suffer them to digge the rocke.

Iamba. "Iamba is an Iland among the Iauas also, from whence come diamants. And the king hath a masse of earth which is golde; it groweth in the middle of a riuer: and when the king doth lacke gold, they cut part of the earth and melt **Golde.** it, whereof commeth golde. This masse of earth doth appeare but once in a yere; which is when the water is low: and this is in the moneth of April.

Bima. "Bima is another Iland among the Iauas, where the women trauell and labour as our men do in England, and the men keepe house and go where they will.[1]

[1] Fitch, who probably heard these accounts of China and Japan and the other places he mentions during his sojourn at Malacca, may here refer to Bima, a seaport town on the island of Sumbawa, Dutch East Indies, now chiefly noted for its export of timber, other produce, and ponies. Iamba, or, in modern spelling, Jamba, possibly represents the present Jambi on the right bank of the river of the same name in the auriferous island of Sumatra. The Dutch founded a factory at Jambi in 1616, and in and around the town many Hindu sculptures have been discovered. If "Laban" represents the island of Labuan on the

He returneth from Malacca.

"The 29 of March 1588, I returned from Malacca to Martauan, and so to Pegu, where I remained the second time vntill the 17 of September, and then I went to Cosmin, and there tooke shipping; and in passing many dangers by reason of contrary windes, it pleased God that we arriued in Bengala in Nouember following: where I stayed for want of passage vntill the third of February 1589, and then I shipped my selfe for Cochin. In which voyage we endured great extremity for lacke of fresh water: for the weather was extreme hote, and we were many marchants and passengers, and we had very many calmes, and hote weather. Yet it pleased God that we arriued in Ceylon the sixth of March, where we stayed fiue dayes to water, and to furnish our selues with other necessary prouision. This Ceylon is a braue Iland, very fruitfull & faire; but by reason of continuall warre with the king thereof, all things are very deare: for he will not suffer any thing to be brought to the castle where the Portu-

Bengala.

Cey on.

north-west coast of Borneo, our traveller's statement will be of interest to the British North Borneo Company, to whom the island, then a Crown colony, was transferred by the British Government about 1890; sago is one of its chief products, and coal mining is carried on with success.

gals be: wherefore often times they haue great want of victuals. Their prouision of victuals commeth out of Bengala euery yere. The king is called Raia, and is of great force; for he commeth to Columbo, which is the place where the Portugals haue their fort, with an hundred thousand men, and many elephants. But they be naked people all of them; yet many of them be good with their pieces which be muskets. When the king talketh with any man, he standeth vpon one legge, and setteth the other foot vpon his knee with his sword in his hand: it is not their order for the king to sit but to stand. His apparell is a fine painted cloth made of cotton wooll about his middle: his haire is long and bound vp with a little fine cloth about his head: all the rest of his body is naked. His guard are a thousand men, which stand round about him, and he in the middle; and when he marcheth, many of them goe before him, and the rest come after him. They are of the race of the Chingalayes, which they say are best kinde of all the Malabars. Their eares are very large; for the greater they are, the more honourable they are accounted. Some of them are a spanne long. The wood which they burne is

Cinamom wood, and it smelleth very sweet. There is great store of rubies, saphires, and spinelles in this Iland: the best kinde of all be here; but the king will not suffer the inhabitants to digge for them, lest his enemies should know of them, and make warres against him, and so driue him out of his countrey for them. They haue no horses in all the countrey. The elephants be not so great as those of Pegu, which be monstrous huge: but they say all other elephants do feare them, and none dare fight with them, though they be very small. Their women haue a cloth bound about them from their middle to their knee: and all the rest is bare. All of

Blacke people.

them be blacke and but little, both men and women. Their houses are very little, made of the branches of the palmer or coco-tree, and couered with the leaues of the same tree.

"The eleuenth of March we sailed from Ceylon, and so doubled the cape

Cape de Comori.

of Comori. Not far from thence, betweene Ceylon and the maine land of Negapatan, they fish for pearles. And there is fished euery yere very much; which doth serue all India, Cambaia, and Bengala, it is not so orient as the pearle of Baharim in the gulfe of Persia. From cape de Comori we passed by

Coulam. Coulam, which is a fort of the Portugals: from whence commeth great store of pepper, which commeth from Portugall: for oftentimes there ladeth one of the caracks of Portugall.[1] Thus passing the coast we arriued in Cochin the 22 of March, where we found the weather warme, but scarsity of victuals: for here groweth neither corne nor rice: and the greatest part commeth from Bengala. They haue here very bad water, for the riuer is farre off. This bad water causeth many of the people to be like lepers, and many of them haue their legs swollen as bigge as a man in the waste, & many of them are scant able to go. These people here be Malabars, and of the race of the Naires of Calicut: and they differ much from the other Malabars. These haue their heads very full of haire, and bound vp with a string: and there doth appeare a bush without the band wherewith it is bound. The men be tall and strong, and good archers with a long bow and a long arrow,

Cochin.

People with swollen legges mentioned also by Ioh. Huygen.

[1] Quilon (Travancore state), one of the oldest towns on the coast, its history going back to the records of the primitive Syrian Church in India. One of the greatest ports of Malabar, it is mentioned as Coilon in a letter of the Nestorian Patriarch Jesujabus who died A.D. 660, and is the Coilum of Marco Polo and the Columbum of several ecclesiastical writers. The Portuguese established a factory and fort here in 1503.

which is their best weapon : yet there be some caliuers among them, but they handle them badly.

How pepper groweth.

"Heere groweth the pepper ; and it springeth vp by a tree or a pole, and is like our iuy berry, but something longer like the wheat eare : and at the first the bunches are greene, and as they waxe ripe they cut them off and dry them. The leafe is much lesser then the iuy leafe and thinner. All the inhabitants here haue very little houses couered with the leaues of the coco-trees. The men be of reasonable stature; the women litle ; all blacke, with a cloth bound about their middle hanging down to their hammes : all the rest of their bodies be naked : they haue horrible great eares with many rings set with pearles and stones in them. The king goeth incached, as they do all : he doth not remaine in a place aboue fiue or sixe dayes : he hath many houses, but they be but little : his guard is but small : he remooueth from one house to another according to their order. All the pepper of Calicut and course cinamom groweth here in this countrey. The best cinamom doth come from Ceylon, and is pilled from fine yoong trees. Here are very many palmer or coco-trees, which is their

Blacke people.

chiefe food: for it is their meat and drinke: and yeeldeth many other necessary things, as I haue declared before.

Or Calicut or Cananor.

"The Naires which be vnder the king of Samorin, which be Malabars, haue alwayes wars with the Portugals. The king has alwayes peace with them: but his people goe to the sea to robbe & steale. Their chief captaine is called Cogi Alli; he hath three castles vnder him. When the Portugals complaine to the king, he sayeth he doth not send them out: but he consenteth that they go. They range all the coast from Ceylon to Goa, and go by foure or fiue parowes or boats together; and haue in euery one of them fifty or threescore men, and boord presently. They do much harme on that coast and take euery yere many foists and boats of the Portugals. Many of these people be Moores. This kings countrey beginneth twelue leagues from Cochin, and reacheth neere vnto Goa. I remained in Cochin vntill the second of Nouember which was eight moneths; for that there was no passage that went away in all that time: if I had come two dayes sooner I had found a passage presently. From Cochin I went to Goa, where I remained three dayes. From Cochin to Goa is an hundred leagues. From Goa I went

Goa.

Chaul. to Chaul, which is threescore leagues, where I remained three and twenty dayes: and there making my prouision of things necessary for the shippe, from thence I departed to Ormus; where I stayed for a passage to Balsora fifty dayes. From Goa to Ormus is foure hundred leagues.

Ormus.

Here I thought good, before I make an end of this my booke, to declare some things which India and the countrey farther Eastward do bring forth.

The pepper tree. The pepper groweth in many parts of India, especially about Cochin: and much of it doeth grow in the fields among the bushes without any labour: and when it is ripe they go and gather it. The shrubbe is like vnto our iuy tree: and if it did not run about some tree or pole, it would fall downe and rot. When they first gather it, it is greene; and then they lay it in the Sun, and it becommeth blacke.

Ginger. The ginger groweth like vnto our garlike, and the root is the ginger: it is to be found in many parts of India.

Cloues. The cloues doe come from the Iles of the Moluccoes, which be diuers Ilands: their tree is like our bay tree.

Nutmegs & maces. The nutmegs and maces grow together, and come from the Ile of Banda, the tree is like to our walnut tree but somewhat lesser.

The white sandol is wood very sweet & in great request among the Indians: for they grinde it with a little water, and anoynt their bodies therewith: it commeth from the isle of Timor.

Camphora. Camphora is a precious thing among the Indians, and is solde dearer then golde. I thinke none of it commeth for Christendome. That which is compounded commeth from China: but that which groweth in canes and is the best commeth from the great Isle of Borneo.

Lignum Aloes. Lignum Aloes commeth from Cauchinchina.

The beniamin commeth out of the countreys of Siam and Iangomes.

Long pepper. The long pepper groweth in Bengala, in Pegu, and in the Ilands of the Iauas.

Muske. The muske commeth out of Tartarie, and is made after this order, by report of the marchants which bring it to Pegu to sell; In Tartarie there is a little beast like vnto a yong roe, which they take in snares, and beat him to death with the blood: after that they cut out the bones, and beat the flesh with the blood very small, and fill the skin with it: and hereof cometh the muske.

Amber.

Of the amber they hold diuers opinions; but most men say it commeth out of the sea, and that they finde it vpon the shores side.

Rubies, saphires and spinels.

The rubies, saphires, and spinelles are found in Pegu.

Diamants.

The diamants are found in diuers places, as in Bisnagar, in Agra, in Delli, and in the Ilands of the Iauas.

The best pearles come from the Iland of Baharim in the Persian sea, the woorser from the Piscaria neere the Isle of Ceylon, and from Aynam a great Iland on the Southermost coast of China.

Spodium.

Spodium and many other kindes of drugs come from Cambaia.

Basora. Babylon. Mosul. Merdin.

"Now to returne to my voyage; from Ormus I went to Balsara or Basora, and from Basora to Babylon: and we passed the most part of the way by the strength of men by halling the boat vp the riuer with a long cord. From Babylon I came by land to Mosul, which standeth nere to Niniue, which is all ruinated and destroyed; it standeth fast by the riuer of Tigris. From Mosul I went to Merdin, which is in the countrey of the Armenians; but now there dwell in that place a people which they call Cordies, or Curdi. From Merdin I went to Orfa, which is a very faire towne, and it hath a goodly fountaine ful of fish; where the Moores hold many great ceremonies and opinions concerning Abraham: for they say he did once dwell there. From thence I went to Bir, and so passed the riuer of Euphrates. From Bir I went to Aleppo, where I stayed certaine moneths for company; and then I went to Tripolis; where finding English shipping, I came with a prosperous voyage to London, where by Gods assistance I safely arriued the 29 of April 1591, hauing bene eight yeeres out of my native countrey."

Bir

Aleppo.

Tripolis.

Homeward bound.

The voyage home from Malacca to London occupied no less a period than three years and one month (March 29, 1588, to April 29, 1591), and the uninterrupted ease with which it was accomplished—after allowing for the inevitable difficulties of travel experienced in those days—affords a marked contrast to the leading incident of the outward journey. Ralph Fitch again joined the increasing crowd of merchants who sailed from one mercantile port to another. From Malacca to Martaban, and thence to Pegu, he pursued his way through the delta to a port in Bengal, probably "Serrepore" (Serampur, see pages 119 and 153); whence he was able to ship to Ceylon. Following the current of commerce he doubled Cape Comorin and, after a call at the famous port of Quilon, he passed several months at Cochin under the very eyes of the Hispano-Portuguese authorities, who were now at open war with his countrymen, and actually stayed a few days at Goa, the scene of his former imprisonment. The journey was continued *viâ* Chaul, Ormuz, Bussorah (Busra), and Bagdad—familiar ground—and then, probably for trading purposes, Fitch, instead of finding the shortest way home, proceeded to visit one or two of the commercial centres of Asia Minor, taking in succession Mosul, Merdin (or Mardeen), and Urfa, which city, by the way, is supposed to be on or near one of the traditional sites of the Ur of the Chaldees. Thence he journeyed, *viâ* Bir (Birejik), across the Euphrates to Aleppo.

Travel-worn, tanned by strange suns, and coming back as one from the dead, Master Fitch must have met with a warm welcome from his fellow Englishmen who were already well-established at Aleppo. Of this he tells us nothing, only stating that he waited here several months for travelling company to Tripolis, where he found English shipping to take him home. It is typical of his modesty that he summarises, in the briefest possible fashion, the details of the later portion of his return journey to the exclusion of all incident. The narrative would have been even more interesting for a few personal touches. It is possible that the hard-headed merchant arrived at the conclusion that his contemporaries would have doubted his whole story had he enlarged upon his own individual adventures and experiences—and he must have seen a good deal of the rough side of

Eastern life in this adventurous epoch As it is, he has at least left us an unvarnished tale, which bears the indelible stamp of truth, and posterity is grateful to one who is proved to have been the sole pioneer of British Empire in the East and Further East.

BOOK IV

BIOGRAPHIES, SIDELIGHTS, AND CONCLUSIONS

JOHN HUYGHEN VAN LINSCHOTEN.

CHAPTER I

RALPH FITCH: HIS FAMILY, COMPANIONS, AND CORRESPONDENCE

Ralph Fitch and the E. I. Company.

UNFORTUNATELY little or nothing of Ralph Fitch's personal history appears to have been preserved, though of the lasting results of his great achievement there is ample evidence. Moreover, to those who are interested in the complex question of heredity, there is the striking fact that two members of his family, after intervals, served their country well in distinguished positions in the distant lands he visited, namely, in India and Burma. Judging by many surrounding circumstances, he appears to have been a retiring man, one who, while fully alive to the probable outcome of his work, was not given to self-advertisement. His name does not appear on the roll of subscribers to the first East India Company even for a moderate sum, and although he was willing to assist the Adventurers by his advice, which must have been most valuable, he does not seem to have been among those chosen to represent them in the negotiations with the Court. There is nothing derogatory in all this; modesty is not incompatible with fixity of purpose and long endurance, nor is it an unknown characteristic of men of action. A curious sidelight is thrown on Fitch's adventure by the following quotation, which exhibits in a few words the interest which was aroused far beyond the circle of merchants and their representatives who were in those lively days making the history of their country: "In 1606 was produced Shakespeare's 'Macbeth': there we read (Act i. scene iii.): 'Her husband's to Aleppo gone, master of the Tiger.' This line, when compared with the opening passage of Fitch's narrative, is too striking to be regarded as a mere coincidence, and is also one of the clearest pieces of evidence known to us of Shakespeare's use of the text of Hakluyt." [1]

As to the active part Master Fitch took in the opening up of the Indian trade, and the esteem in which he was held by the influential men who were determined upon the stupendous enterprise, we have only two recorded instances, but they are eloquent enough. At a meeting of Adventurers, which Mr. Richard Staper and Mr. John Eldred attended, held on the (2) 1st of October, 1600, the year of the Charter, the appended resolution was adopted :—

"It is alsoe orderid that the said m Ald^n^ Bannyng Captein Lancaster m Allabaster together wth m Eldred and mr. ffitche shall in ther meeting to morrowe morning at m Allabasters house conferre of the merchaundize fitt to be

[1] "Dictionary of National Biography."

pvided for the viage and to (make) sett downe their opinions of the said merchaundize that the same may be presentid to these Comittees at ther next meeting to be further resolved vponn."[1]

The following, dated December 31, 1606, is the last known incident in the history of Master Ralph Fitch; it shows that he survived his pioneering journey for at least fifteen years, and took part in the affairs of the East India Company down to the third voyage:—

"Court Minutes of the East India Company. Present: Sir William Romney, Governor, Sir Thos. Smythe, Sir Thos. Cambell, Wm. Harrison, Robt. Johnson, Reynold Greene, Robert Bucke, Humphrey Smyth, Sir Jas. Lancaster, Geo. Boles, John Highlord, John Eldred, Robert Coxe, Robt. Sandye, and Hugh Hamersley. Victuals to be provided for the third voyage. Letters to be obtained from King James to the King of Cambaya, the Governors of Aden, and two more places not far from Aden; their titles to be inquired of Ralph Fitch; also letters to be sent as from His Majesty to those Kings who sent him presents. The destination of each ship to be decided upon. Names of factors appointed to the Dragon, Hector, and Consent. Fras. Bucke promised to adventure £100. Bonds to be given by each factor; their request to employ stock in the voyage."[2]

[1] "The Dawn of British Trade to the East Indies as recorded in the Court Minutes of the East India Company, 1599–1603," by Henry Stevens of Vermont, with an introduction by Sir George Birdwood, p. 26.

[2] Sainsbury's "Calendar of State Papers, East Indies, 1513–1616." No. 356.

William Fytche.

The interesting circumstance that two members of a family which Ralph Fitch had already distinguished should have attained eminence in widely separate portions of the British-Indian Empire is further enhanced by the fact that one of them, the late Lieut.-Gen. Albert Fytche, has left the story on record.[1] He tells us that William Fytche, who was in the service of the East India Company, was appointed a member of the Council of Merchants at Calcutta in 1746, and in 1749 became Chief of the English factory at Cossimbazaar, the fort and mart of Moorsherabad, at that time the native capital of Bengal. In January, 1752, he was appointed President of Fort William, but died on August 10th from dysentery, aged thirty-five years. "It is a strange circumstance," he adds, "that during the same year of 1752 Warren Hastings was sent from Calcutta to fill a subordinate post at Cossimbazaar. He must have arrived there a few weeks after the departure of William Fytche for Calcutta." The soldier-author publishes a fine portrait of the President of Fort William: he describes it as follows, with an accompanying diatribe which, to say the least, is pardonable: "A portrait of William Fytche was painted by Hogarth; it has been preserved in the family. It was not taken from life, but was painted from a

[1] "Burma, Past and Present," by Lieut.-Gen. Albert Fytche, C.S.I., late Chief Commissioner of British Burma and Agent to the Viceroy and Governor-General of India, 2 vols (Kegan Paul, 1878). The book is dedicated to "My Cousin Alfred Tennyson, Poet Laureate."

sketch taken in Bengal, and a portrait by a native artist. The picture is suggestive. It is difficult to look at it without thinking what a part William Fytche might have played in the subsequent history of India had he not been cut off by that cruel dysentery, which is the curse of Bengal. He was succeeded by Roger Drake. When Suraj-ood-dowlah invested Calcutta, Roger Drake declared he was a quaker, and escaped on board a ship with the ladies. The costume of William Fytche shows that he was no quaker. I may be permitted to believe that had William Fytche been President of Calcutta in 1756 Suraj-ood-dowlah would have returned to Moorsherabad at a much earlier date than is recorded in history. I am also inclined to believe that there would have been no 'Black Hole' tragedy, although possibly there might have been a battle of Plassey." We are further assured that it is a good likeness, as it strongly resembles a larger picture of his brother Thomas painted by Hudson about the same time.

The following note will speak for itself: "In those days the rate of exchange was very different from its present lamentable state. From family papers I perceive that William Fytche used to send remittances home to his brother Thomas Fytche of Danbury Place, Essex, by Government Bills of Exchange, drawn at ninety days after sight, at two shillings and fourpence each rupee."

Albert Fytche.

In his interesting contribution to Burmese history Lieut.-Gen. Fytche tells us he "landed in India as a young Ensign in 1839; I left it as Chief Commissioner of

British Burma in 1871. With the exception of two years at starting, and a few occasional intervals, I spent the whole of this period of thirty-two years in the province of British Burma." Dilating on the differences of the Indian journey in 1839 from what they are in later times, the author says that embarkation was regarded almost as a lifelong separation, adding as an illustration a set of four verses written on his departure by his youthful cousin Charles Tennyson (who afterwards took the name of Turner), brother of the poet laureate, and addressed to his mother. Fytche, who was then barely eighteen years of age, had as a fellow-passenger on the ship *Marquis Camden*, the famous John Nicholson, a lad of sixteen. He was appointed Chief Commissioner of British Burma and Agent to the Viceroy in 1867, in succession to Major-Gen. Sir Arthur Phayre, who was the first Commissioner, and served the term of four years.

John Newberie, pioneer and trader.

The leader of the Fitch expedition on its setting forth from London in 1583 was an experienced traveller and courageous pioneer. This much we can gather from the records of the three voyages he undertook, including the last one to India, but, as in the case of Ralph Fitch himself, we know little more about him. When the three English adventurers separated at Fatehpur Sikri in September, 1585, it will be remembered Newberie set off for Lahore, announcing his intention of returning through Persia to England, whence he would send a ship to Pegu. From this we may gather that he was highly satisfied with the result of the mission, and saw great possibilities in the Eastern trade for his countrymen and co-partners. There is one suggestion of doubt as to his return home, which is dealt with below.

The first of his journeys of which we have an account was to the Holy Land, and this is all that Purchas give us. It contains in the opening sentences a very interesting hint of the Protestantism of the writer—that is, assuming that the few words in question are not an interpolation by the Rev. Samuel Purchas himself:—

"I Iohn Newberie Citizen and Merchant of London, desirous to see the World, the eighth of March, 1578, according to the computation of the Church of England, began a Voyage from the Citie of London to Tripolie in Syria, and thence to Ioppe and Hierusalem, and the Countrey round about adioyning, which I performed in passing through France to Marceils, where I embarqued my selfe, and passing through the Leuant or Mediterranne Sea, arriued in Tripolie the thirteenth day of May; and within few dayes after at Ioppe, and thence at Hierusalem, and the chiefe places thereabout: And spending a moneth in visiting the Monuments of those Countries, I returned to Ioppe the tenth of Iune, 1579. And the fifteenth of the said moneth arriued againe in Tripolie; from whence shortly after I visited Mount Libanus, and returning speedily to the said Port of Tripolie, I embarqued my selfe in a ship of Marceils, the first of Iulie, and the three and twentieth of the said moneth, I put in at Candia; and the seuenth day of September, arriued safely in Marceils, and passing through France by Lions, Paris, Roan and Diepe. The tenth of Nouember of the aforesaid yeere 1579 by Gods helpe arriued safely in London."

Appended is the introduction to the second voyage, the success of which accounts for Master Fitch's introductory statement that Newberie had already been at Ormuz :—

"I the said Iohn Newbery being incouraged by the prosperous successe of my former Voyage to Tripoly, Hierusalem, and Mount Lybanus, vndertooke a farre more long and dangerous voyage, by the Straights of Gibraltar, the Mediterranean Sea, the aforesaid Tripoly, and downe the River of Euphrates, as farre as the Citie of Ormus in the Gulfe of Persia, and from thence through the Countrey of Lar, and the most Easterne parts of Persia to Media, Armenia, Georgia, Carmania, Natolia, and so to Constantinople, and from thence by the Blacke Sea, called in the old time *PontusEuxinus*, into the Mouth of the River Danubius by shipping, and so a great way vp the said River, passing by the parts of Bugdania and Valachia, at length landing, I came to Caminetz, the first Frontier Towne of Poland; and passing through that Kingdome, arriued in Prussia, and came to Elbing, and Dantzk, and Quinsborow, where imbarquing my selfe, I passed through the Sound of Denmark, and arriued at Hull in England and so ouer land trauelled to London, whither I came the last day of August, 1582, making my voyage in the space of two yeeres, lacking nineteene days."[1]

As evidence of Newberie's energy it will be noticed that although he only returned from his "farre more long and dangerous voyage" in August, 1582, he set off again to India in 1583. One cannot forego the conclusion that in fact he was an instigator as well

[1] Both voyages are from Purchas, book ix. chap. iii.

as the personal director of the Indian scheme. In his interesting detailed narrative of the second voyage he says he left London in the good ship *White Hinde*, on September 19, 1580, and, in relating his experiences at Ormuz, tells a curious tale and introduces the rival trader Michael Stropene, who, during the Fitch voyage, did so much to hinder or baulk the English expedition. For some reason which he does not explain, his travelling companions, about a score in number and of various nationalities (not including English), all made oath that Newberie was a Christian of Aleppo, "and had wife and children and a house there." He adds, "The seuenth day of Iulie, my man Iacomo, which was a Greeke, went from me to one Michael Stropene a Venetian, being as I suspect, entised thereunto by him, to vnderstand my secret purposes." Purchas here prints the following passage: "and in very deed, in my last Voyage to these parts, in the year 1583, this Michael Stropene betrayed me and my companie to the Gouernor of Ormus." For the moment the sentence raises the curious question as to the time when Newberie wrote the account of his second voyage. There is every reason to believe that he never returned from the expedition to India, Purchas himself assumes as much, and it is inconceivable that he wrote the long detailed narrative of the second voyage amid the arduous trials of the third in order to send it home.[1] The only possible conclusion is

[1] Purchas, book x. chap. vi., in a marginal note to Fitch's narrative of the Indian journey, says of Newberie, "in which he seemeth he died, vnknown how or where." A less direct refer-

that the sentence was added by another hand, and that the editor, in his desire to give point to Newberie's own story, was not scrupulous as to the means he adopted.

Further light is thrown upon the character of this remarkable man, who was of the best type of the Elizabethan Englishman, by the letters he sent home. His last missive, to Master Leonard Poore, of London, appears in an earlier chapter (pages 71 to 81). Others written during the last journey are give here.[1] The first discloses in a highly interesting manner the intimate relations in which the Rev. Richard Hakluyt stood to the leading explorers and travellers among his countrymen, and how he availed himself of their services in the work he loved and carried out so well; it also fills in one or two details of the voyage:—

"Right welbeloued, and my assured good friend, I heartily commend me vnto you, hoping of your good health, &c. After we set saile from Grauesend, which was the 13. day of

ence, but one which does not disturb the theory that Newberie never returned to England from Fatehpur Sikri, appears in the 1626 edition, p. 579 ("Pilgrimage"): "John Newbury which sayled downe Euphrates to this Sea (Persian Gulf) and so to Ormuz (visiting Bagdet by the way, which he saith is twentie or five and twentie miles, Southward from old Babylon) testifieth of the women in Ormuz, that they slit the lower part of their eares more than two inches, which hangeth downe to their chin. This our Countreyman dyed in his Trauels, having trauelled to Constantinople, into the blacke Sea, and Danubius, and through the Kingdomes of Poland and Persia, the Indies, and other parts of the World."

[1] Hakluyt, vol. ii. part i.

February last, we remained vpon our coast vntill the 11. day of March, and that day we set saile from Falmouth, an neuer ankered till we arriued in the road of Tripolie in Syria, which was the last day of Aprill last past, where wee stayed 14 days; and the twentie of this present we came hither to Alepo, and with Gods helpe, within fiue or sixe dayes goe from hence towards the Indies. Since my comming to Tripolis I haue made very earnest inquirie both there and here, for the booke of Cosmographie of Abilfada Ismael, but by no meanes can heare of it. Some say that possibly it may be had in Persia, but notwithstanding I will not faile to make inquirie for it, both in Babylon, and in Balsara, and if I can finde it in any of these places, I wil send it you from thence. The letter which you deliuered me for to copy out, that came from M. Thomas Steuens in Goa, as also the note you gaue mee of Francis Fernandes the Portugal, I brought thence with me among other writings vnawares, the which I haue sent you here inclosed. Here is great preparation for the warres in Persia, and from hence is gone the Bassa of a towne called Rahemet, and shortly after goeth the Bassa of Tripolis, and the Bassa of Damasco, but they haue not all with them aboue 6000. men from hence, and they goe to a towne called Asmerome, which is three dayes iourney from Trapezunde, where they shal meete with diuers captaines and souldiers that come from Constantinople, and other places thereabout, which goe altogether into Persia. This yeere many men goe into the warres, and so hath there euery yeere since the beginning thereof, which is eight yeeres or thereabouts, but very fewe of them returne againe. Nothwithstanding, they get of the Persians, and make castles and holds in their countrey. I pray you make my hearty commendations to master Peter Guillame, and master Philip Iones, and to M. Walter Warner, and to all the rest of our friends. Master Fitch hath him heartily commended vnto you: and so I commit you to the tuition of the Almightie, who blesse and keepe you, and send vs a ioyfull meeting. From Alepo, the 28. of May 1583.

"Your louing friend to command in all that I may,

"IOHN NEWBERIE."

The two following letters, sent to Master Poore, breathe the true spirit of the merchant-adventurer of the age:—

"Right welbeloued, my very heartie commendations vnto you, and the rest of my friends remembered. My last I sent you was the 25. of February last, from Dele out of the Downes, after which time with contrary windes wee remained upon our owne coast, vntill the 11. day of March, and then wee set saile from Falmouth, and the thirteenth day the winde came contrary with a very great storme, which continued eight days, and in this great storme wee had some of our goods wette, but God bee thanked no great hurt done. After which time we sailed with a faire wind within the Streights, and so remained at Sea, and ankered at no place vntil our comming into the roade of Tripolis in Syria, which was the last day of April. This was a very good passage. God make vs thankfull for it. The foureteenth day of this present wee came from Tripolis, and the twentieth day arriued here in Alepo, and with the helpe of God to morrowe or next day, wee beginne our voyage towards Babylon and Balsara, and so into India. Our friend Master Barret hath him commended to you, who hath sent you in the Emanuel a ball of Nutmegs for the small trifles you sent him, which I hope long since you haue receiued. Also hee hath by his letter certified you in what order hee solde those things, whereof I can say nothing, because I have not seene the accompt thereof, neither haue demaunded it: for euer since our comming hither hee hath bene still busie about the dispatch of the shippe, and our voyage, and I likewise in buying of things here to cary to Balsara, and the Indies. Wee haue bought in currall for 1200. and odde ducats, and amber for foure hundreth ducates and some sope and broken glasse, with all other small trifles, all which things I hope will serue very wel for those places that wee shall goe vnto. All the rest of the accompt of the Barke Reinolds was sent home in the Emanuel, which was 3600. ducats, which is 200. pound more then it was rated. For master Staper rated it but 1100. li. and it is 1300. pound, so that our part is 200. pound. Besides such profit as it shall please God to sende thereof: wherefore you shall doe very well to speake to M. Staper for the accompt.

"And if you would content your selfe to trauell for three or foure yeeres, I would wish you to come hither or goe to Cairo, if any goe thither. For wee doubt not if you had remained there but three or foure moneths, you would like so well of the place, that I thinke you would not desire to returne againe in three or foure yeeres. And, if it should be my chance to remaine in any place out of England, I would choose this before all other that I know. My reason is, the place is healthfull and pleasant, and the gaines very good, and no doubt the profit will bee hereafter better, things being vsed in good order: for there should come in euery ship the fourth part of her Cargason in money, which would helpe to put away our commodities at a very good price. Also to haue two very good ships to come together, would doe very well: for in so doing, the danger of the voyage might be accompted as little as from London to Antwerpe. Master Giles Porter and master Edmund Porter, went from Tripolis in a small barke to Iaffa, the same day that we came from thence, which was the 14 day of this present, so that no doubt but long since they are in Ierusalem: God send them and vs safe returne.

At this instant I haue receiued the account of M. Barret, and the rest of the rings, with two and twentie duckats, two medines in readie money. So there is nothing remaining in his hands but a few bookes, and with Thomas Bostocke I left certaine small trifles, which I pray you demaund. And so once againe with my hearty commendations I commit you to the tuition of the almightie, who alwayes preserue vs. From Aleppo the 29 of May 1583.

"Yours assured,

"IOHN NEWBERIE."

"My last I sent you, was the 29 of May last past from Aleppo, by George Gill the purser of the Tiger, which the last day of the same moneth came from thence, & arriued at Feluge the 19 day of Iune, which Feluge is one dayes iourney from hence. Notwithstanding some of our company came not hither till the last day of the last moneth which was for want of Camels to cary our goods: for at this time of the yeere, by reason of the great heate that is here, Camels are very scant to be gotten. And since our comming hither we haue found very small sales, but diuers say that in the winter our commodities will be very well sold, I pray God their words may prooue true. I thinke cloth, kersies & tinne haue neuer bene here at so low prices as they are now. Notwithstanding, if I had here so much readie money as the commodities are woorth, I would not doubt to make a very good profite of this voiage hither, and to Balsara, and so by Gods helpe there will be reasonable profite made of the voiage. But with halfe money & halfe commoditie may be bought here the best sort of spices, and other commodities that are brought from the Indies, and without money there is here at this instant small good to be done. With Gods helpe two dayes hence, I minde to goe from hence to Balsara, and from thence of force I must goe to Ormus for want of a man that speaketh the Indian tongue. At my being in Aleppo I hired two Nazaranies, and one of them hath bene twise in the Indies, and hath the language very well, but he is a very lewde fellow, and therefore I will not take him with me.

"Here follow the prices of wares as they are worth here at this instant.

"From Babylon the 20 day of Iuly 1583,

"Yours,

"IOHN NEWBERIE."

Two more letters from Newberie have been preserved by Purchas, who says they were found among the papers of "M. William Hareborne, Her Maiesties Embassador to the Grand Signior at Constantinople," a statement which opens up a wide field of conjecture as to the relations of our pioneer Eastern travellers with the diplomatic representatives we were then establishing abroad. They are dated respectively Babylon, July 15, 1583, and Balsara, August 15, 1583, and give some details of the progress of the journey and the prospects of trade. In taking leave of Master John Newberie no excuse is needed for again expressing regret that he did not survive to tell his complete story for the benefit of his countrymen, not only of his own time, but of ours.[1]

Thomas Stevens, S.J., missionary pioneer.

It will be remembered that when the four Englishmen—Newberie, Fitch, Leedes, and Storie—arrived as prisoners at Goa they found a countryman who had preceded them. This was Thomas Stevens, or Stephens, a member of the Jesuit Order—the first Englishman (of whom there is a record) to double the Cape of Good

[1] Purchas, vol. ii. p. 1642–3.

Hope, and the first to reach India by any route. Father Stevens was born at Buston (? Boscombe), in the diocese of Salisbury, about 1550. In early life he was associated with Thomas Pounde—whose various imprisonments, extending over thirty years, as an English recusant, fill an eloquent page in Roman Catholic martyrology—and proceeding to Rome was admitted among the novices of St. Andrea, in 1575. Four years later, in April, 1579, Stevens sailed with a fleet of five ships from Lisbon, arriving at Goa on October 24th. A lively account of the voyage, in a letter written by the young Jesuit to his father shortly after his arrival, is preserved in Hakluyt (vol. ii. part ii.). He tells how an "English shippe" set upon his vessel, which had become separated from the rest of the fleet off Madeira, but, after firing a few shots, drew off when the Portuguese had got ready their "greatest ordinance." As to the hardships of the journey, which he says was prolonged to nearly seven months, instead of the usual five, because they had started late in the season, scurvy appears to have become prevalent in the fleet; they had one hundred and fifty sick, of whom twenty-seven died, "which losse they esteemed not much in respect of other times." His missionary labours extended over a period of more than forty years, during which he was for some time Rector of Salsette. He died at Goa in 1619 in the seventieth year of his age.

It has been suggested that the letters sent home by Thomas Stevens first drew the attention of his countrymen to the great possibilities of trade with India; there is, however, no hint of the kind in the one referred to above.[1] But he interested himself in the lot of wandering Englishmen and other foreigners, who met with anything but a welcome from the Portuguese authorities at Goa. Two or three accounts of what he did, or suggestions of the influence he exercised, in the case of Fitch and his companions have been given in a former chapter. Pyrard of Laval, the French traveller, who found himself cast into prison with other unfortunates at Goa about 1609, speaks with gratitude of the action of several Jesuit Fathers, including "Thomas Estienne, rector of a college in the Salsete territory." Personally, Father Stevens appears to have been an ideal missionary in relation to both Europeans and natives, and his life and character stand out in strong contrast to his general surroundings. It is stated that he was the first to make a scientific study of Canarese. "His familiarity with the dialects of the country is proved by his having published three works—a Konkani Grammar, an Account of Christian Doctrine, and a History of Christ, which he called a Purana."[2]

Linschoten, traveller and geographer.

John Huyghen van Linschoten, the famous Dutch traveller and geographer, was born at Haarlem about 1563, in the

[1] See Newberie's reference, p. 207.

[2] "The Voyage of François Pyrard of Laval," vol. ii. p. 269, by Messrs. Albert Gray and H. C. P. Bell (Hakluyt Society). Foley's "Records of the English Province of the Society of Jesus," vol. iii. p. 573 *et seq.* Prof. Monier Williams, *Contemporary Review*, April, 1878. The latter adds: "I find that one Thomas Stevyns took his degree at St. John's College, Oxford, in June, 1577." Hakluyt describes Father Stevens as formerly of Oxford.

midst of the troublous period of the Spanish occupation of the Low Countries. Some ten years later, about the date of the siege and sack of Haarlem—one of the most striking episodes in the history of the Netherlands—the family removed to the seaport of Enkhuizen, which had early declared for William of Orange. The lad thus cradled, as it were, in the din of battle, was able in after years to do yeoman's service for the cause of freedom, at any rate from a commercial standpoint, and to take a leading part in that revolution which eventually wrested the glorious East from the hold of Spain. He was of that methodical, courageous, and withal stubborn stock which could persistently and successfully resist oppression; which sent forth explorers and navigators who rivalled those of Spain, Portugal, and England in the early days; which has at the present time its representatives in distant lands, both East and West, who are being shouldered, perhaps, by more modern-spirited competitors, but who still preserve qualities worthy of due regard and honourable acknowledgment. When he was about fourteen years of age, John, who was of a roving disposition, went to join his two brothers, who were apparently established as traders in Spain; for, notwithstanding the political and religious disturbances, commercial relations were maintained between the two countries, which, nominally at least, were under the same crown. Here the young adventurer, whose bright intelligence and keenness of observation were ere long to place his contemporaries, as well as posterity, under a deep debt of gratitude, learnt the Spanish language, and eventually one of his brothers, who was engaged as clerk or purser in the Indian fleet, obtained for him an appointment in the suite of Fonseca, the new Archbishop of Goa. The two brothers sailed with the Archbishop from Lisbon in April, 1583 (Fitch's year of departure), arriving in September at Goa, where John remained five years. During his sojourn Fitch and his companions were brought prisoners to the Eastern emporium, and the part he took in assisting them has already been related. The Archbishop died on his way to Europe in 1587, and on the news reaching India in 1588 Linschoten, who found himself out of employment, determined to return home. Leaving Goa at the end of 1588 or beginning of 1589, the Portuguese fleet of five or six vessels arrived in the Azores in July, and, in order to escape the English cruisers, was obliged to anchor before Tecera, with disastrous results, for at this time of the year it was dangerous to lie there. Linschoten remained here two years or more, and became very friendly with the Governor. He took advantage of the opportunities thus afforded him to explore the island and write a description of it; he was further enabled to add an account of the occurrences in the Azores to the end of 1591, including the death of Richard Grenville. In 1592 he returned to Lisbon, whence he proceeded to his home at Enkhuizen the same year.

If John Huyghen Van Linschoten had been satisfied with the *rôle* of an adventurer we should probably have heard little or nothing about him, but he commenced at once to put to some practical and enduring service the results of his wanderings and his personal inquiries. By the beginning of 1596 he had completed his "Itinerario," but portion of it appeared in 1595, and is said to have been in use on board the ships forming the first Dutch expedition to India. The whole work proved of immense value to the seafarers and explorers of that adventurous epoch. The first part consisted of the description of the East and his own itinerary; the second part (published first) dealt with routes to the East, Far East, and the American coasts, compiled from the best existing sources, besides an account of the domains, tributes, &c., of the King of Spain; the third went into descriptions of the African coasts, and further details were given concerning America. There were no less than six large maps in the original edition, besides many plates and plans, and the ready recognition of the high importance of the "Itinerario" may be gauged by the fact that translations in English and German were published in 1598, two in Latin in 1599, and one in French in 1610, to say nothing of reprints. Linschoten at this time showed the liveliest interest in the search for a north-east passage to India and China, in which he was a firm believer, and he took part in two Dutch expeditions in that direction. He afterwards became treasurer of the town of Enkhuizen, where, among other literary labours, he assisted his friend Wagenhaer in the production of what have been described as "the best sailing directions of that time." In 1610 he applied to the States-General for a pension in view of the services he had rendered his country, but the application was refused on the ground that he received sufficient emolument from the patents

JOHN ELDRED.

granted him for his own books which were renewed that year. He died on February 8, 1611, at the comparatively early age of forty-eight years.[1]

John Eldred, merchant and traveller.

This famous London merchant, the friend, travelling companion, and correspondent of Fitch and Newberie, was born at New Buckenham, Norfolk, in 1552. The family was of Suffolk origin, and John, having made his fortune in Eastern trade, returned thither and purchased the manor of Great Saxham, near Bury St. Edmunds. Here he built a large house, which came to be known in the locality as "Nutmeg Hall," doubtless in allusion to the foundation of its proprietor's wealth. The first occasion on which he comes into prominence as merchant-adventurer is in connection with his journey to Tripoli, Bagdad, and Bussorah, his trading experiences at Aleppo, and his visit to the Holy Land. Eldred set out with Fitch and Newberie and other merchants in the *Tiger*, 1583, and reached the Thames on his return in 1588, "in the *Hercules* of London, which was the richest ship of English marchants goods that euer was knowen to come into this realme." Eldred supplied Hakluyt with a graphic account of his five years' experiences abroad, in which he refers to the calamity to those of the party who continued the journey to India. Purchas also gives three letters of Eldred's, which (as in the case of the two from Newberie, see *ante*) he says were found among Hareborne's papers at Constantinople. The first, dated Bagdet, July 14, 1583, deals with the arrival and plans

[1] A biographical sketch of Linschoten is given in the Hakluyt Society's edition of his travels.

for the future. The second, Balsara, November 6, 1583, signed by Eldred and Shales, is of great interest. It tells us that Newberie's pathetic appeal for help, sent "from out the prison at Ormuz" in September, had been forwarded express to Aleppo; moreover, it settles the question of Newberie's capital (as leader of the expedition) in money and goods for the Indian voyage. Eldred fixes it at £400 (£2,400 present value), which is a much less sum than the Dutch Jesuit at Goa said the travellers had in their possession, even assuming that Fitch had a similar amount. In the third letter, also signed by Eldred and Shales, dated Balsara, January 22, 1583 (4), the following appears: "We received no Letters from Master Newberie since the first newes of his trouble: but we heare by others that he and his Companie are sent Prisoners to Goa, and the remayner of his goods is left in the hands of the Kings Factor."

Eldred took an active part in the formation and subsequent operations of the East India Company. His name appears in the first list of subscribers for £400, and in the roll of the first Court of Directors. His busy life came to a close in 1632, and he was interred in the church of St. Andrew, Great Saxham. The body lies near the altar, and his bust stands in a niche on the south side. "Above are the arms of Eldred, with a martlet in chief Gules, for difference." In the pavement of the church is a black marble table of an altar tomb, in the centre of which is a brass bearing an engraved effigy of Eldred in his alderman's gown. Along the verge are brasses bearing the arms of Eldred and Rivet (he married Mary

Rivet, or Revet, of Risbroughs, Suffolk), the City of London, and the Clothworkers and Russia Companies. A brass plate underneath the bust is inscribed :—

MEMORIÆ SACRUM.
Iohn Eldred
New Bvchingam in Norfolke was his first
Being. In Babilon hee spent some parte
Of his time, and the rest of his earthly
Pilgrimage hee spent in London, and was
Alderman of that Famous cittie.
His age } LXXX.
His death }

The holy land so called I have seene,
And in the land of Babilon have bene
Bvt in yt land where gloriovs saints doe live
My sovle doth crave of Christ a roome to give,
And theire with holy angells Halilviahs singe
With Ioyfvll voyce too God ovr heavenly King
No content bvt in the O Lord.

On the tomb are three plates with inscriptions in Latin and English. The latter runs as follows :—

Might all my travells mee excvse
For being dead and lying here ;
Or if my riches well to vse
For life to death might mee endeare ;
I had my fate or quite ovtgone
Or pvrchase't death's compassion.
But riches can no ransome bvy
Nor travels pass ye destiny.[1]

[1] For Eldred's voyage, Hakluyt, vol ii. part i. See also Gage's "History and Antiquities of Suffolk, Thingoe Hundred," and "Dictionary of National Biography." In Page's "Suffolk Traveller" it is stated that "Nutmeg Hall" was burnt down in 1779, the present mansion being completed in 1798.

CHAPTER II

THREE MEN OF THE TIME

WHILST posterity is so deeply indebted to the men of action who ventured their lives in opening up the remotest parts of the world to their countrymen, a meed is due to those others whose wealth and wide views of commercial policy enabled them, to a very large extent, to suggest and encourage the various enterprises of the period. The expedition to India, as Fitch frankly tells us, was "chiefly set foorth" by Sir Edward Osborne and Master Richard Staper, citizens and merchants of London. By singular coincidence the journey was undertaken in the same year that Osborne was knighted and elected Lord Mayor, while Fitch returned in the year that saw the termination of his highly successful career (1591). There seems to be no evidence that Osborne and Staper were actually associated in permanent commercial partnership, but we have proof enough that they had warm sympathies in common, and that they liberally expended their means to develop the Eastern trade. At the present time, after a lapse of

Photo] [*London Stereoscopic Co.*

SIR EDWARD OSBORNE.

Lord Mayor, 1583-4.

nearly three centuries, their visible mementoes are preserved in the City of London, almost within bow-shot of each other. The copy of the painting of Sir Edward Osborne, now in the possession of the Duke of Leeds, hangs in the court-room of the Clothworkers' Hall, Mincing Lane, close by the stern lineaments of his father-in-law, Sir William Hewet (or Hewitt); while in the ceiling-arch of a division wall in the drawing-room of the same sumptuous building is Beverley's picturesque design representing the brave deed by which young Osborne laid the foundations of his fortune, and of a name destined to rank with the proudest in the land. In the church of St. Helen, Bishopsgate, hard by, is the monument of his friend and associate, Richard Staper, of which an excellent engraving is preserved in the hall.

Sir Edward Osborne, Lord Mayor.

Born about 1530, the son of Richard Osborne, of Ashford, Kent, Edward came to London when a mere boy, for the incident which was the turning-point in his career would appear to have occurred before his formal apprenticeship to Sir William Hewet (Lord Mayor in 1559). It is recorded that Hewet's infant daughter was dropped by her nurse from the window of an apartment in his house on London Bridge, when young Osborne plunged into the river and saved the child. "The date of this event," says one authority, "must have been about 1545, as the lady, who became Osborne's wife, was twenty-three years old at the time of her father's death in January, 1566–7." According to the "Gregory Collection" among the archives at Clothworkers' Hall, Sir William Hewet, the wealthy merchant, took the lad as an apprentice in May, 1547; the same series contains the definite statement that Anne Hewet was born in 1543. Edward Osborne was not only taken into the favour of his rich and influential employer, but was given the girl he had rescued in marriage when she was about eighteen years of age. She was the sole heir of her father, whose estate, it was estimated, was then worth £6,000 a year. She had many suitors, including the Earl of Shrewsbury, but Sir William —whose notions of rectitude, though carried to an extreme in this instance, were amply justified by the event—curtly replied, "Osborne saved her, and Osborne should enjoy her." The following note appears in the collection already referred to:—

"The gallant action of Sir Edward Osborne with reference to the daughter of Sir William Hewitt, noticed by Stowe and other historians, has been the subject of a graphical record, there is a small but rather uncommon engraving of him leaping from the window of Sir William's House on London Bridge executed from a drawing by Saml. Wate. As this artist died in the year 1786 it is of course but little authority as a representation of the fact but nevertheless interesting as giving a portraiture of the dwellings on London Bridge in his time, and with this print may also be mentioned one designed by the same hand and engraved by Charles Grignion, of the first Duke of Leeds pointing to a portrait of Sir William Hewet's daughter and relating to King Charles the 2nd. the foregoing anecdote of his ancestor. It will be found in Guthrie's complete History of the Peerage of England having vignettes at the conclusion of the history of each family."

DESIGN SHEWING OSBORNE'S RESCUE OF ANNE HEWET.

Edward Osborne made rapid progress in commercial and public life. He became a freeman of the Clothworkers' Company, May 8, 1554; Alderman of Castle Baynard Ward, 1573; was Sheriff 1575–6; and Lord Mayor 1583–4. He was knighted February 2, 1583, and elected M.P. for London 1586. As a matter of civic interest, it is recorded of him that he was "the first Lord Mayor who nominated citizens to the office of Sheriff by drinking to them;" and this touch of originality may be taken as typical of other more solid instances of his lively interest in City affairs, which have been left on record, and which resulted in his being returned to Parliament. The State Papers contain numerous examples of his activity, both as citizen and merchant or financial agent. His various enterprises in the development of foreign trade, when the merchant prince could communicate direct with the sovereign, are repeatedly referred to by Hakluyt, from whom we learn that Sir Edward had command of at least one foreign language—namely, Spanish. His interest in the formation of the Levant or Turkey Company has already been mentioned; the following concise extract will throw further light upon it:—

"This trade into the Leuant was very vsuall and much frequented from the yeere of our Lord 1511, till the yeere 1534, and afterwards also, though not so commonly, vntill the yeere 1550, when as the barke Aucher vnder the conduct of M. Roger Bodenham made a prosperous voyage vnto Sicilia, Candia, Sio, and other places within the Leuant. Since which time the foresaid trade (notwithstanding the Grand Signiors ample priuilege granted to M. Anthony

Ienkenson 1553, and the strong and weighty reasons of Gaspar Campion for that purpose) was vtterly discontinued, and in maner quite forgotten, as if it had neuer bene, for the space of 20 yeares and more. Howbeit the discreete and worthy citizens Sir Edward Osborne and M. Richard Staper seriously considering what benefite might grow to the common wealth by renuing of the foresaid discontinued trade, to the inlarging of her Maiesties Customes, the furthering of nauigation, the venting of diuerse generall commodities of this Realme, and the inriching of the citie of London, determined to vse some effectuall meanes for the reestablishing and augmenting thereof.

"Wherefore about the yeere 1575 the foresaid R. W. marchants at their charges and expenses sent Iohn Wight and Ioseph Clements by the way of Poland to Constantinople, where the said Ioseph remained 18 monethes to procure a safe conduct from the grand Signior, for M. William Harborne, then factor for Sir Edward Osborne, to haue free accesse into his Highnes dominions, and obtained the same.

"Which businesse after two yeres chargeable trauell and suit being accomplished, the sayd M. Harborne the first of Iuly 1578 departed from London by the sea to Hamburgh, and thence accompanied with Ioseph Clements his guide and seruant, he trauelled to Leopolis in Poland, and then apparelling himselfe, his guide, and his seruant after the Turkish fashion (hauing first obteyned the king of Poland his safe conduct to passe at Camienijeez the frontier towne of his dominions next vnto Turky) by good means he obteined favour of one Acmet Chaus the Turks ambassadour then in Poland, and readie to return to Constantinople, to bee received into his companie and carouan. And so the fourth of September 1578 he departed with the said Acmet from Leopolis in Poland, and trauelling through Moldauia, Valachia, Bulgaria, and Romania, gratifying the Voiauodes with certaine courtesies, he arriued at Constantinople the 28 of October next insuing. Where he behaued himselfe so wisely and discreetely, that within few moneths after he obtained not onely the great Turkes large and ample priuiledge for himselfe, and the two worshipfull persons aforesaid, but also procured his honourable and friendly letters vnto her Maiestie in maner following:"[1]

As the founder of a distinguished family, Sir Edward Osborne had issue by his wife, Anne Hewet, two sons and three daughters—Sir Hewet Osborne, born 1567, and knighted by the Earl of Essex in Ireland; Edward, who was a barrister of the Inner Temple and died unmarried, 1625; Anne, wife of Robert Offley of London; Alice, married to Sir John Peyton of Isleham, Kent, Knight and Baronet; and Jane, married to John Webley in the Isle of Ely. Sir Edward was afterwards married, but had no further issue, to Margaret, the daughter of Sir John Maynard, who survived him and intermarried with Robert Clarke, one of the Barons of the Exchequer. So far as can be judged from the meagre records which have been preserved, Sir Edward Osborne was a typical citizen and Lord Mayor, active and enterprising to a degree in commercial and financial life, jealous of the civic privileges, and morally beyond reproach. He died in February, 1591, and was buried in St. Dionis Backchurch, Fenchurch Street, on the 16th of that month. The following was the monumental inscription in the south aisle of the choir of

[1] Hakluyt, vol. ii. part i. p. 136. The letter of Sultan Murad, dated March 15, 1579, and Queen Elizabeth's reply of October 25th, are given in full.

the church, which was destroyed in the Great Fire of 1661 :—

M. H. I. C.

Christe duce, & ossa resurgent

> The Tombe of Sir Edward Osborne, Kt. some time Lord Maior of this Noble Citie, who was buried An. Dom. 1591. and of Dame Margaret his second Wife, Who married after with M Baron Clarke, (by whom this Tombe was erected) and was Buried An. Dom. 1602.

But the romance of the brave boy of London Bridge, the 'prentice who married his master's daughter, and eventually succeeded him as Lord Mayor; the merchant and financier, who lent his powerful aid and devoted his untiring energies in those distant days to lay the foundations of our Empire in the East, is not yet complete. His extraordinary qualities, courage, and enterprise were continued by his son, Sir Hewet Osborne, who gained his title for gallantry in the field against the Irish rebels. The next in line, Sir Edward Osborne, Bart., rendered conspicuous service to Charles I., and his son Sir Thomas—the great-grandson of Sir Edward Osborne the Lord Mayor—was raised to the peerage, by patent from Charles II., in August, 1673, as Viscount Latimer and Baron of Kiveton in the County of York, being created Earl of Danby and Viscount Dumblane the following year. Lord Danby is one the most prominent figures in the history of this period and during the troublous times when James II. was king. He is credited with taking an active part in arranging the marriage of the Princess Mary with William of Orange, and after the Revolution William III. advanced him to the dignity of Marquis of Carmarthen (1689); in 1694 he was created Duke of Leeds. The title at the present day is not unworthily borne by George Godolphin Osborne, M.P. for the Brixton Division 1883–96, Assistant Secretary to the Colonial Secretary 1887–8, and Treasurer of her Majesty's Household 1895–6.[1]

Richard Staper, merchant.

Full of energy and enterprise as he undoubtedly was, there appears to have been nothing left on record concerning the personality of this successful Elizabethan merchant. That he did not limit his ventures to the Levant and the East generally appears from a letter written to him by one John Whithal from Santos, Brazil, in 1578. The latter explains that he has delayed his return home owing to the fact that "it is in this countrey offered me to marry, and to take my choice of three or foure." Master Whithal eventually fixed his affections on the daughter and only child of a Genoese sugar planter, who made over as dowry

[1] The "Gregory Collection," at Clothworkers' Hall, contains several interesting incidents of Sir Edward Osborne's Shrievalty and Mayoralty, copies of his signature, and quotations from Stow's "Survey"; also an assortment of extracts relating to the family history, and two fine engravings of Sir Thomas Osborne as the Earl of Danby, after Lely, and as the first Duke of Leeds, from Vander Vaart. The National Portrait Gallery contains a print of the great Duke, in Garter robes, drawn and engraved from the life by Robert White. A quaint account of the London Bridge story is repeated in Mr. R. Thomson's "Chronicles of London Bridge," pp. 313–16.

a share in an "Ingenio," which turned out a large quantity of sugar yearly, with the promise of the management of the whole business, including sixty or seventy slaves.[1] It seems strange that none of the published letters sent home by Fitch and Newberie during their voyage were addressed to either Osborne or Staper, the prime movers in the undertaking; it is possible that these astute merchants received private intelligence which they did not choose to communicate to Mr. Hakluyt.

Staper, who is described as of Plymouth and London,[2] was a member of the Merchant Taylors' Company, and as early as 1574 was appointed by the Crown on a Commission for the discovery and plantation of new settlements in America.[3] Mr. Henry N. Stevens, in his preface to the volume of Court Records, makes the interesting statement that a number of letters he reproduces, which are probably draft letters of the Company of Levant Merchants, were found in the manuscript volume containing the first minutes of the East India Company, having been commenced at the other end of the book. From the dates of the entries he suggests that the book was for a time used in common by both Companies, and that one Company grew out of the other, for several persons mentioned appear to have been members of both.[4] Staper was a vigorous member of both Companies.

[1] Hakluyt, vol. iii. p. 701.

[2] Fox Bourne's "English Merchants," vol. i. p. 199.

[3] Clode's "Early History of the Merchant Taylors' Company," vol. i. p. 322.

[4] Stevens's "Dawn of British Trade to the East Indies."

Photo] [*London Stereoscopic Co.*

MONUMENT TO RICHARD STAPER,
St. Helen's, Bishopsgate

With regard to the larger adventure, and in fact the foundation of the East India Company, Staper's name appears repeatedly in various forms, from Stap to Stapers, in the volume of minutes which extends from 1599 to 1603. At the beginning, under the heading: "The names of such persones as haue writtin withe there owne handes, to venter in the pretended voiage to the East Indias (the whiche it maie please the Lord to psper) and the Somes that they will adventure the xxij September 1599," Master Staper is down for £500, and the total reached was £30,133 6s. 8d. At an assembly of adventurers two days later it was decided to limit the subscriptions to a minimum of £200 so far as new comers were concerned, but Staper, who was a member of the General Committee, increased his contribution, and by August 28, 1601, his "Bill of Adventure" was sealed at £800.

Sainsbury continues the record from the Court minutes. Thus in September, 1607, we find that Mr. Staper is returned as a debtor to the Company; in June, 1608, the month and year of the veteran adventurer's death, it is recorded that one John Mednoll writes from the Indies "to his master Rich. Staper," offering his services to the Company for £1,500 "in hand." In October, 1609, "Hewett, son of Richard Staper, merchant," is admitted to the Company; the Christian name of the new member is suggestive of his father's connection with the Osborne family. The last time that the name "Stapers" occurs in the calendar, at any rate in the early years of the history of the East India Company, bears the date August 19, 1614, when it is stated: "Newman employed by Mr. Stapers, Abbott and others, to recover goods from John Midnall who died at the King's Court at Adsmere (Ajmere). There is some hope of getting the goods." The Midnall, or Mednoll, referred to was sent out by Richard Staper, as we have already seen, and thus we have evidence that to the end of his days this enterprising merchant was at work, by means of his agents, in developing the Eastern trade.

In the church of St. Helen, Bishopsgate, on the north wall of the nave, is an elaborate mural monument, which was removed from St. Martin's Outwich, now pulled down, in 1874. It bears the following inscription :—

Here Resteth the Bodie of the Worshipfvl Richard Staper Electid Alderman of this Cityc Anno 1594. Hee Was the Greatest Merchant in His Tyme: the Chiefest Actor in Discovere of The Trades of Tvrkey and East India. a man hvmble in Prosperity, Paynefvl and ever ready in the Affayres Pvbliqve and Discreetly Careful of His Private. A Liberal Howsekeeper. Bowntifvl to the Poore: An Vpright Dealer in the World. and A Divovt Aspirer after the World to Come. mvch blest in His Posterity. and Happy in His and their Alliances. He Dyed the last Jvne, Anno Domine 1608 Intravit vt Exirit

Richard Hakluyt, father of modern geography.

The list of correspondents and personal associates of Fitch and Newberie would be incomplete without some brief reference to one whose enthusiastic industry has preserved for us the story of their journey. Born in 1553 in Herefordshire, of a family supposed to be of Dutch origin, Hakluyt was educated at Westminster School, and having been elected to a studentship at Christ Church, Oxford, proceeded to his degree and took holy orders. His love of geography is said to have been kindled by a cousin of the same name, a member of the Middle Temple, and such was his ardour that he mastered no less than six languages in order to be able to peruse all the narratives of travel and adventure he could procure, afterwards lecturing on these subjects. It is said of him, by one who has every authority to speak on such a topic, that he "began to see two great needs of his country, and set himself to work with patriotic zeal to remedy the evils. The first was caused by the ignorance of our seamen as regards the scientific branch of their profession. The second was the absence of records, and the way in which important voyages and travels were allowed to fall into oblivion. He strove, during a long life, with great ability and untiring perseverance to remedy these evils; and the measure of success he attained justly places his name among those of worthies who have deserved well of their country."

In 1582 he published "Divers Voyages touching the Discovery of America," which has been described, not inaptly, as our "first impetus to colonisation." He proceeded to Paris the following year, as Chaplain to Sir Edward Stafford, English Ambassador. Pursuing his inquiries in this new sphere Hakluyt, in 1584, produced "A Particular Discourse concerning Western Discoveries," which was followed in 1587 by his translation of Laudonnière's Journal and "De Orbe Novo Petri Martyris Anglerii, Decades Octo, illustratæ labore et industriâ Ricardi Hakluyti." Having been given the reversion of a prebendal stall at Bristol by the Queen, to which he succeeded in 1586, he returned to England in 1588, and the next year appeared his "Principall Navigations," published in a single volume and dedicated to Sir Francis Walsingham. Appointed to the rectory of Wetheringsett, Suffolk, in 1590, Hakluyt devoted himself to the production of his great work in three volumes, bearing a title almost identical in terms to the one just mentioned. The first appeared in 1598 (with a corrected title-page in 1599), and the series was completed in 1600. He laboured at his task with enthusiastic devotion. "Nothing could stop or daunt him when there was a chance of obtaining new information. He rode 200 miles to have an interview with the last survivor of Master Hore's expedition to America in 1536. He saved numerous journals and narratives from destruction and the deeds they record from oblivion. His work gave a stimulus to colonial and maritime enterprise, and it inspired our literature. Shakespeare owed much to Hakluyt's 'Principal Navigations'; Milton owed much more. He declared geography and chronology to be the sun and the moon, the right eye and the left of all history." In 1602 Hakluyt was appointed prebendary of Westminster, and became archdeacon the following year. In 1604 he was one of the chaplains of the Savoy. The last of his publications was a translation from the Portuguese of the travels of Ferdinand de Soto, which appeared in 1609 under the title of "Virginia Richly Valued."

But besides his untiring energy in collecting and translating materials for his invaluable books, we have ample evidence that Richard Hakluyt continued to put forth every effort in furtherance of the work about which he wrote so much for the benefit of his countrymen. That he was on terms of intimacy with the travellers and explorers themselves we have already had one instance, in the letter written to him by Newberie from Aleppo. His wide knowledge and timely advice contributed much to the successful foundation of the East India Company. One or two extracts from the First Minute Book, as reproduced by Stevens, speak for themselves. Hakluyt's name first appears as "Hacklett," under date October 16, 1599, when he attended a meeting of the "Committees," Richard Staper being present. The next entry giving his name is on January 29, 1600:—

"Mr. Hacklett the historiographer of the viages of the East Indies, beinge here before the Comitties and having read vnto them out of his notes and bookes divers instruccons for provisions of Jewelles, was required to sett downe in wryting a note of the principall places in the East Indies wher Trade (was) is to be had to thend the same may be vsed for the better instruccon of o^{r} factors in the said voyage."

The following interesting minute is recorded on February 16, 1600, and this appears to be the last reference to Hakluyt in the books of the Company:—

"Ther is geaven to Mr. (Ald^{r}) Hackett by thassent of this assemblie for his travelles taken in instruccons and advyses touching the preparing of the voyage and for his former advyses in setting the voyage in hand the Last yere the somme of ten poundes and xxx^{s} for 3 mappes by him provided and dd to the companie the same money to be p^{d} him by Mr Ald. Hollyday."

During the last years of his life his attention appears to have been chiefly directed to the Virginian colonisation scheme. He was one of the chief promoters of the petition for patents addressed to James I. in 1606; his book on the subject, as already mentioned, was published in 1609, and he was a leading adventurer in the London, or South Virginia, Company. Richard Hakluyt died on November 23, 1616, and was interred at Westminster Abbey; he was twice married, in or about 1594 and in 1604. Up to the time of his death Hakluyt appears to have been engaged in the work for which posterity owes him so much gratitude. He left a large collection of manuscripts, most of which came into the hands of the Rev. Samuel Purchas, of St. Martin's, Ludgate Hill, whose "Pilgrimes" was published with "Hakluytus Posthumus" on the title-page, and, notwithstanding sundry faults, have proved a mine of literary wealth.[1]

[1] For the bibliography of Hakluyt see "Dictionary of National Biography." The quotations are from the address of Sir Clements Markham, F.R.S., President, at the fiftieth anniversary meeting of the Hakluyt Society, December 15, 1896.

SPANISH ARMADA ATTACKED BY FIRESHIPS.

CHAPTER III

HISTORICAL SUMMARY, 1583–91[1] — DECLINE OF PORTUGAL IN THE EAST—SPAIN AND THE PHILIPPINES — COMING OF THE DUTCH — BEGINNING OF BRITAIN'S EMPIRE

DURING the eight years' absence of Master Ralph Fitch public affairs in Europe, and the work of adventure, exploration, and expansion by his own countrymen, had been making rapid progress. In the year after his departure, 1584, the infamous ban issued by Philip of Spain against the Prince of Orange took effect, and William the Silent fell by the hand of the assassin Balthasar Gerard. The shock

[1] The episode in the long fight with the Spanish Armada which is reproduced on the opposite page is from a volume in large folio, which may be seen in the Print Room of the British Museum. It is entitled: "The Tapestry Hangings of the House of Lords representing the several engagements between the English and Spanish Fleets in the ever memorable year MDLXXXVIII., with the portraits of the Lord High Admiral, and the other Noble Commanders, taken from the Life," &c.; a series of charts is added, and an account of each day's action "from the most Authentic Manuscripts and Writers." The work was published in 1739 by John Pine, engraver, who was

caused in England by this outrage was intensified by the discovery of the Throgmorton Conspiracy to murder the Queen and to place Mary of Scots upon the throne, which was immediately followed by the rupture of diplomatic relations with Spain and the expulsion of the ambassador Mendoza. Thus at last the two countries became open enemies. Antwerp, the great commercial centre to which much of the growing Eastern trade had been attracted, fell before Alexander of Parma in 1585, after a memorable siege, and the Earl of Leicester was sent to the help of the Netherlands on a futile expedition, which is chiefly remembered for the death of his nephew, Sir Philip Sidney, at Zutphen, in 1586. Another elaborate conspiracy against Elizabeth's life, in which Mary of Scots was implicated by the ever-watchful Walsingham, was then made public. It appears to have been hatched at Rheims, and Anthony Babington, who had charge of the scheme in England, was executed in 1586, Mary herself being brought to the block in 1587. Meanwhile Drake had been busy. In 1585 he left Plymouth, with Frobisher as a lieutenant, to

informed that "the Designs of the Tapestry were made by Henry Cornelius Vroom, a famous Painter of Harlem, eminent for his great Skill in drawing of all Sorts of Shipping : and that it was Wove by Francis Spiring." The tapestries were involved in the great fire which wrecked the Houses of Parliament in 1834, a circumstance which lends additional interest to Mr. Pine's fine collection. Each engraving, with its border of portraits, covers two pages of the volume, and as to the one now reproduced the compiler quotes Camden to the effect that eight fire-ships were sent among the Spaniards off Calais and caused a panic.

harry the Spanish colonies; he set off again in 1587 to carry out his famous exploit against Spain itself, and to "singe the beard" of Philip who was preparing for his great attack on England. The year 1588 witnessed Spain's *débâcle*. The "Invincible Armada" set forth in May, 1588—to return in broken fragments, typical alike of the collapse of Philip's worldwide ambitions and the beginning of Britain's claim to the supremacy of the sea.

"Virginia." It is remarkable that in the interval of eight years no further attempt was made by the English to tap the riches of the Golden East, though the final crippling of the Spanish sea power was quickly followed by incursions direct into the Eastern seas, as is related below. But there was no lack of enterprise in the North and West, and even an attempt at colonisation. The Queen in 1584 issued letters patent to Raleigh, similar in terms to the charter granted to Gilbert referred to in an earlier chapter, and in that year he despatched two small ships to explore from the coast of Florida northwards. They returned the same year, and in 1585 Raleigh sent a larger expedition under Richard Grenville, with Ralph Lane as governor of the new colony of Virginia, which was to be established on the shores of North Carolina, one of the party being Thomas Cavendish, who was afterwards to become famous as the second English circumnavigator. Little but disaster and misrule, however, attended the enterprise, and in 1586 Drake, on his return from the West Indies expedition of 1585, brought Lane and his colonists home. Soon afterwards Grenville arrived with supplies, and finding the island of Roanoke deserted by his countrymen, left fifteen men, well provisioned, to hold the settlement. A fourth expedition was sent out by Raleigh, under Captain White, in 1587, the latter being again despatched in 1590, but it was not till the formation of a new company in 1606 that the successful colonisation was actually begun. Concurrently with these efforts John Davis had been pursuing the quest for a northerly route to Cathay. He completed his three years' voyages to the North West in 1585–6–7, but no further attempt to reach the Far East by steering a northerly course was made during the Queen's reign, with the exception of an abortive expedition in 1602 undertaken by one George Waymouth at the joint charge of the newly formed East India Company and the Muscovy Company. In 1588 Cavendish had completed his voyage round the world. In 1591 he sailed again on his last and unfortunate expedition, during which he died of a broken heart, Davis, the navigator, returning with the remnants of his party in 1593.

Portuguese in the East—past and present.

"In 1640," remarks Hunter in his historical summing-up (vol. vi.), "Portugal again became a separate country. But in the meanwhile the Dutch and English had appeared in the Eastern seas; and before their indomitable competition the Portuguese empire of the Indies withered away as rapidly as it had sprung up. The period of the highest development of the Portuguese Commerce was probably from 1590 to 1610, on the eve of the subversion of their commercial power by the Dutch, and when their political dominion in India was at its lowest depth of degradation. . . . The only remaining Portuguese posessions in India are Goa, Daman, and Diu, all on the west coast, with a total area of 2,365 square miles." It is not the purpose here to deal with all the colonial possessions of Portugal in Africa and elsewhere, but to the Eastern and Far Eastern list we must add Macao, the only established centre of their commerce which Master Fitch did not visit. This brings up the roll to four places, which affords a miserable comparison with the claims put forward by the historian Faria y Sousa in an addendum to his third volume. "The Portuguese Empire to the Eastward," he says, "extends from the Cape of Good Hope in Africk, to Cape Liampo in China, distant from one another 4000 Leagues along the Seacoasts, without including the shores of the Red Sea and Persian Golph, which make about 1200 Leagues. Between this space lies half Africk, and all Asia with innumerable Islands adjoining to those vast Parts of the World." He divides the whole region into seven parts, and in each case enumerates the actual Portuguese settlements and bishoprics. As to the last two he states: "The sixth Division between Ganges and Cape Singapura, contains the vast Kingdoms of Bengala, Pegu, Tanazarim, and others of less Note. Here we have the City Malaca, a Bishop's Seat, and the last place we possess in the Eastern Continent. The seventh Division between the Capes Singapura and Liampo, contains the Kingdoms of Pam, Lugor, Siam, Cambodia, Tsiompa, Cochinchina, and vast

Empire of China. Here we have no place but the City Macao yet Trade all along those Coasts."

At Macao, at present little more than a pleasure resort, and, indeed, a nest of gamblers, the Portuguese were permitted by the Chinese to erect factories as early as 1557. The Jesuits having established themselves at the settlement, Gregory XIII. constituted a bishopric of Macao in 1580; a senate was organised in 1583, and in 1628 Jeronimo de Silveira became the first royal governor. The Chinese suzerainty, however, was not thrown off till 1849. "One classic memory, however, may save Macao from oblivion. It was here that the exiled Camoens composed the greater part of his *Lusiads*. On one of the hillsides overlooking the bay is an extensive old shrubbery, where narrow paths twist in and out among gnarled and ancient trees, and where half a dozen enormous boulders heaped together form a natural archway or grotto—the *Gruta de Camões*. Camoens was appointed *Provedor dos defuntos e ausentes*—Commissary for the Defunct and the Absent—in Macao, and is supposed to have come here every day to work at his great task." A bronze bust of the poet was erected in 1840.[1]

Spain as an interloper.

It will be interesting here to recall the fact that the Spaniards made an early appearance in the Eastern seas on their own account. Magellan, in his circumnavigation, discovered the Philippines in 1521, and lost his life there shortly after his arrival. When the news reached Europe that the celebrated voyager

[1] "Peoples and Politics of the Far East," p. 189.

LEGAZPI, CONQUEROR OF THE PHILIPPINES.

had appeared in the Moluccas, and that conflicts had occurred between the Spanish and Portuguese in that region, a quarrel arose between Spain and Portugal. The Bull of Alexander VI. was produced by both sides, but eventually, by an agreement made at Saragossa, April 22, 1529, Spain sold her claim to her rival for 350,000 ducats of gold, but retained the right of pre-emption. But the Portuguese, although they insisted on their monopoly of the spice trade, never got a firm grip of the group, which eventually came into the hands of the Spanish. In 1543 Villalobos sailed to the islands from Mexico, and was the first to suggest the present name by calling Samar Filipina, while in 1565 Legazpi founded the settlement of San Miguel at Cebu; in a letter of Legazpi's of 1567, it is stated, the name Islas Filipinas appears for the first time. The English captured Manila in October, 1762, and proceeded to subjugate the province. Attacked by the Hispano-Tagal forces, they were hemmed in at Manila and were nearly reduced by famine, when peace was declared, the town being restored in March, 1764.[1]

The Dutch in the East.

"The Dutch were the first European nation who broke through the Portuguese monopoly," says Hunter. To begin with, they, like the English, endeavoured to get to Asia by following a northern course, and it will be remembered that Linschoten was associated

[1] Danvers's "Portuguese in Asia," vol. i. chap. xiv.; also "The Philippine Islands," edited for the Hakluyt Society by Lord Stanley of Alderley, in which appears the portrait of Legazpi.

with their earlier efforts in that direction. But the rapid developments of this historical period—with the disastrous policy of Spain as the primary cause—turned their attention to the bolder course of following the Cape route, with which their indefatigable countryman had made them familiar. There was the further circumstance that their chief ports had become the European centres for the Indian trade. Danvers says that when Antwerp fell before the attacks of the Duke of Parma in 1585 this circumstance, coupled with its disastrous experiences of Spanish occupation and pillage, brought about commercial ruin and the transfer of trade to Amsterdam and Hamburg, "a fact which the Dutch did not fail to realise."[1] Hunter, in his usual terse fashion, puts it: "During the sixteenth century Bruges, Antwerp, and Amsterdam became successively the great emporiums where Indian produce, imported by the Portuguese, was distributed to Germany, and even to England." Thus, while the Dutch were not the first Europeans to send a rival fleet to India *viâ* the Cape—we refer to Lancaster's voyage in 1591, dealt with in the next division—they were the first to undertake the enterprise on systematic lines.

In 1594 a company, called the Company of Foreign Merchants, was formed in Holland, and Cornelius Houtman, with a fleet of four ships, left the Texel at the beginning of 1595. This Dutch pioneer-navigator reached Bantam, and returned with three of his vessels,

[1] "Letters Received by the East India Company from its Servants in the East," by Mr. F. C. Danvers; introduction (Sampson Low, 1896).

richly laden with spices and other produce, in 1597. Several other companies were set on foot for trade with the East—in fact before Houtman's return another expedition was sent out under the command of James Van Neck. It is a remarkable fact that two celebrated Englishmen took leading parts in these early efforts of the Hollanders. In 1598, when Houtman set forth on his second expedition, in which he lost his life, John Davis accompanied him as chief pilot. The same year a fleet of five ships left Rotterdam with William Adams, the first Englishman to visit Japan, on board as pilot-major. By 1602 the States-General had decreed the amalgamation of the various companies in the United Provinces into the Dutch East India Company.

The appearance of the Dutch in the Eastern seas bore immediate fruit in the shape of constant conflicts with the Portuguese, which developed into a fierce rivalry with the English. The manner in which they pushed their way through the crumbling pretensions of Portugal during the twenty years which followed Houtman's first voyage is a feature of the history of this most active period. Danvers, in the work just quoted, states: "Towards the end of the year 1613 the Dutch already had factories and castles in the following ports:—viz., Bantam, Jakatra, Grasse, Succadana, Macassar, Patani, Siam, Achin, Bouton, Amboyna, Bakean, Makjan, Motir, Tidore, Ternate, Japan, Bandar, and Solor. . . . The English at this time could boast of no other properly established factory than that at Bantam, although they did carry on an uncertain trade in the Moluccas and at places in Sumatra. . . . On the peninsula of India also the English were prevented from taking advantage of the opportunities that presented themselves owing to a want of means." Taking a wider range, Hunter gives us a still more comprehensive view of the brilliant, if comparatively short, record of their supremacy in the East and on the way thither. "Within fifty years," he says, "the Dutch had established factories on the continent of India, in Ceylon, in the Persian Gulf, and in the Red Sea, besides having obtained exclusive possession of the Moluccas. . . . During the seventeenth century the Dutch were the foremost maritime power in the world. Their memorable massacre of the English at Amboyna in 1623 forced the British company to retire from the Eastern Archipelago to the continent of India"—a result, it is pointed out, which led to the foundation of that Indian Empire which exists to-day.

As in the case of Portugal, a comparison between the present Eastern possessions of the Netherlands and what they promised to be two centuries or more ago affords ample ground for reflection. The possessions and protectorates of the kingdom of Holland in the archipelago include, among other islands, Java and Madurá, Sumatra, parts of New Guinea, and of Borneo, the Moluccas and Celebes. But the most friendly critic would now find it difficult to become enthusiastic in regard to the administration of these thickly populated and fertile "colonies." In India and Ceylon the Dutch flag is not seen at all, though there are traces of their settlements at various places—for instance, Chinsurah, Negapatam, and Jaffnapatam.

It must not be forgotten that they discovered Australia, and that to this day the passage between Ceylon and the Indian peninsula still bears the name of a Dutch governor, Palk.

Lancaster's first voyage to India.

"The defeat of the Spanish Armada appears to have greatly stimulated English maritime enterprise, by inspiring the people with additional confidence in their national superiority at sea; and in October, 1589, less than one year after that event, a body of English merchants memorialised the Queen for permission to send ships to trade with India."[1] The outcome, apparently, was the Raymond expedition which sailed from Plymouth on April 10, 1591—nineteen days before Fitch arrived in London from his own perilous journey. The fleet consisted of three tall ships: the *Penelope*, commanded by Captain George Raymond, who had charge of the enterprise; the *Merchant Royal*, Captain Abraham Kendal; and the *Edward Bonaventure*, Captain James Lancaster. The story of this voyage, which is of so much interest to the British of the present day, was told to Hakluyt (vol. ii. part ii.) by Edmund Barker of Ipswich, Lancaster's lieutenant; another account, by one Henry May, is preserved in Purchas's "Pilgrimes."[2] Beaten about by adverse winds, they

[1] Danvers, "Letters," introduction.

[2] Both narratives appear in "The Voyages of Sir James Lancaster to the East Indies," edited by Mr. (now Sir) Clements R. Markham for the Hakluyt Society. Barker's version is followed in the above summary, but it may be added that May states that Samuel Foxcroft was captain of the *Merchant Royal*

did not come in sight of the Cape till the end of July, when, in order to refresh the crews, many of whom were "weake and sicke," they put into an adjacent bay on the eastward side, the Agoada (watering-place) de Saldanha.[1] Here it was decided to send back the *Merchant Royal* with fifty men, "whereof there were many pretty well recovered," and continue the journey with those who were "sound and whole"—that is, unaffected by the scurvy. The *Penelope*, with one hundred and one men, and the *Edward* with a complement of ninety-seven, again set sail in company, but not for long. On September 14th, when off Cape Corrientes, they encountered a great storm, in which the *Penelope* (Captain Raymond) disappeared and was never seen again. Thus Captain Lancaster was left to proceed on the voyage alone or to return. He chose the former course, and entered upon a series of privateering adventures in the Bay of Bengal and among the Nicobars which rivalled the exploits of Drake in the West Indies. There was one feature of Lancaster's proceedings, however, which acquits him of the charge of common piracy. In the account before us it is stated that when a vessel which was seized was found to be owned, or laden, by others than the Portuguese it was allowed to go unmolested.

In December, 1592, the *Edward Bonaventure* found her way back to the Point de Galle, Ceylon, where

and second in command of the expedition, and that there was a fourth vessel in the shape of a "small pinesse"—possibly used for victualling purposes and then abandoned.

[1] Markham (p. 62) states that Saldanha Bay of De Barros and the Early English and Dutch navigators is our Table Bay.

Lancaster intended to lie in wait for the Bengal Fleet. But he was attacked by sickness, and the crew having become weary of their wanderings, it was determined to sail for home—a voyage which was to prove utterly disastrous. A pathetic incident occurred on their arrival at St. Helena. Here they found one John Legar (or Segar) of Bury, Suffolk, who had been left behind by the *Merchant Royal* to recover from severe illness. The man had become half-demented, and the unexpected appearance of his countrymen appears to have brought about a condition of excitement which proved fatal to him within a few days. On leaving the island contrary winds and unknown currents carried the *Edward* across the Atlantic, and a course was set to find the Isle of Trinidad to re-provision. After a series of arduous adventures among the West Indian islands, the *Edward*, as she lay one night in November, 1593, off the Island of Mona (between Puerto Rico and San Domingo), either broke away or was cut adrift with five men and a boy aboard. Meanwhile Henry May appears to have been sent to England on a French ship, and thus there were left on the island Captain Lancaster and eighteen men—the miserable remnant of the ninety-seven who sailed eastward from the Cape. Barker accounts for the whole number. Twelve were taken by two French vessels to San Domingo, seven who had wandered into the island being left behind. Soon afterwards a vessel of Newhaven appeared at San Domingo with two of the seven, reporting that three had been killed by the Spaniards, and two had broken their necks in trying to catch fowls on the cliffs. Captain Lancaster and Lieutenant Barker, leaving the rest of their crew, who seem to have been well treated on the other French ships, to follow, took passage in a vessel commanded by a Captain la Noe for Dieppe. They then crossed to Rye, where they landed on May 19 1594, after an absence of over three years. Thus ended the first English voyage, *viâ* the Cape, to India.[1]

Another independent venture to the Indian seas took place in 1596, principally at the cost of Sir Robert Dudley, the fleet consisting of three vessels, the *Bear*, the *Bear's Whelp*, and the *Benjamin*, under the supreme command of Captain Benjamin Wood. Sainsbury tells us that Queen Elizabeth entrusted a letter for the Emperor of China to two merchants who joined the expedition, Richard Allen and Thomas Bromfield. The last heard of this fleet seems to have been contained in a letter received by Cecil from Lisbon, in September, 1598, which stated that news had come to hand that two English ships "in the India" had taken two Portuguese ships, rich in treasure, on their way from Goa to China ; the writer "supposes it is Captain Wood in Mr. Dudley's ships."

Captain James Lancaster, whose pioneer voyage round the Cape is briefly recorded above, was conspicuous among the maritime adventurers of the time. Little is known of his early days, but he is said to

[1] A still earlier attempt is related in "A Forgotten Voyage of John Davis," contributed by Mr. W. Foster to the *Geographical Journal*, August, 1893. The navigator sailed with one John Sanderson in the *Samaritan* for India in September, 1590, but got no further than Madeira.

have been a native of Basingstoke, and to have spent some time in Portugal both as soldier and merchant. Returning to England before the definite outbreak of war with Spain, he commanded the *Edward Bonaventure*, described as of 300 tons, serving under Drake against the Spanish Armada. Soon after his Indian adventure, in fact within a month or two of his home-coming without his ship, Lancaster was entrusted with the general command of three vessels, fitted out by the merchants and aldermen of the City of London for a privateering expedition against Pernambuco, which proved highly successful. His next and last voyage was in command of the first fleet despatched by the East India Company. On his return in 1603 he was knighted. One of the first directors of the Company, he henceforward took a most active part in its affairs, and appears to have been held in high esteem. Baffin gave his name to one of the Sounds in the frozen north-west. Sir James died in May or June, 1618.[1]

Foundation of our Indian Empire.

The next, and, as to its permanent results, the last stage in laying the foundations of our Indian Empire was the formation of the first East India Company. Some account has been given in preceding chapters of both men and methods in the earliest days of the association of merchants and navigators for commerce with the East and Far East. The time had now come for prompt action. Sir George Birdwood writes: "In

[1] "First Letter Book of the East India Company," edited by Sir George Birdwood, assisted by Mr. William Foster, p. 2 (Quaritch, 1893). "Dictionary of National Biography."

1599, the Dutch, who had now firmly established their trade in the East, having raised the price of pepper against us from 3s. per lb. to 6s. and 8s., the merchants of London held a meeting on the 24th September 'at Founders' Hall,' under the Lord Mayor, and agreed to form an association for the purpose of establishing direct trade with India. Queen Elizabeth also sent Sir John Mildenhall by way of Constantinople to the Great Mogul to apply for privileges for the English Company, for whom she was then preparing a charter; and on the 31st December, 1600, the English East India Company was incorporated by Royal Charter under the title of the Governor and Company of Merchants of London trading into the East Indies."[1] An incident which is very suggestive is recorded by the same authority. When, in 1592, some English privateers captured the great Portuguese carrack *Madre de Dios*, and brought her into Dartmouth, they found amongst their plunder "The Notable Register or Matricola of the whole Government and Trade of the Portuguese in the East Indies." It was on this unique document that the memorial to the Queen in 1599 was founded. In his "Lancaster" (p. 2) Markham gives the following as one of the immediate incentives in the formation of the Company: "In 1599, the full report of Dr. Thorne, who resided at Seville, on the advantages of a trade with India, and other information, including that obtained by Lancaster during his first voyage, induced the merchants and adventurers

[1] "Report on the Old Records of the India Office," p. 179 (W. H. Allen and Co., 1891).

of London to project an expedition, and eventually to form a Company, with the object of establishing a trade with the East Indies." It may be fairly claimed that the "other information" comprised the fruits of the labours, foresight, and actual travel, of such men as Osborne and Staper, Eldred, and Hakluyt, and last, but not least, Ralph Fitch.

The first voyage undertaken by the Company, 1601–3, was under the command of the indomitable Lancaster, with John Middleton, who died at Bantam, 1603, as second in command. It consisted of five vessels, the *Mare* (or *Malice*) *Scurge*, which was re-christened the *Red Dragon*, the *Hector*, *Ascension*, *Great Susan*, and the much smaller vessel *Guift*, or *Guest*, which was used as a store-ship. John Davis, who had already made the voyage to the East Indies under the Dutch pioneer Houtman, embarked as chief pilot. Some interesting figures have been collated in regard to the fleet. The *Mare Scurge*, 600 tons, was bought from the Earl of Cumberland for £3,700 (then value) and manned with a complement of 200, the *Hector* had 100 men, the *Great Susan* (which cost £1,600) 80 men, and the *Ascension* 80 men; while the *Guest* cost £300.[1] The first twelve voyages down to 1612, known as the "Separate" voyages, were undertaken at the risk of the sub-

[1] Markham furnishes slightly different figures as to the tonnage and the manning of the vessels (p. iv). He adds the interesting statement that Davis received a "bill of adventure," which was to bring him £500 if the voyage yielded two for one, £1,000 if three for one, £1,500 if four for one, and £2,000 if five for one.

scribers, but, in view of the increasing competition with the Dutch and Portuguese, the Company then decided that they should be made as joint-stock enterprises. The first "joint-stock" fleet of four vessels, Downton in command, was despatched in 1613, and Sir Thomas Roe proceeded on his famous embassy to Jehangir, the son of Akbar, in 1615.[1] All the "Separate" voyages, excepting the fourth, were very prosperous, the clear profits hardly ever being below 100 per cent., and in general yielding an average of 138. In spite of the opposition of the Dutch, the returns on the four voyages of the first "joint-stock" account amounted to 87½ per cent. on the subscribed capital.[2] "This period of purely commercial operations may be divided into three well-marked sub-periods: the first from 1600 to 1623, the date of the 'Massacre of Amboyna,' during which the Company pushed its trade in the East Indies under the greatest difficulties, but without exciting much popular attention; the second from 1623 to 1660, during which, partly in consequence of the national solicitude aroused by the massacre of the Company's agents at Amboyna, a general competition was rapidly developed throughout the country for a participation in the commerce of the East Indies;

[1] See "The Embassy of Sir Thomas Roe to the Court of the Great Mogul," by Mr. William Foster (Hakluyt Society, 1899).

[2] The figures are from Birdwood's "Report," and Sainsbury in the "Calendar" furnishes many interesting details as to the preparations and proceedings of the Company. Danvers, in his "Letters" (introduction), mentions that the clear profits on the first two voyages amounted to 95 per cent., and on the third to no less than 234 per cent.

and the third and last, from 1660 to 1709, during which this disastrous rivalry at length resulted in the amalgamation of the 'London,' or 'Old,' and the 'English,' or 'New,' Companies, in the 'United Company of Merchants of England trading into the East Indies,' commonly known as the Honourable East India Company; whose great commercial Empire was sequestrated to the British Crown in 1858."[1]

This brief record of how modern England came to possess her Indian heritage would be incomplete without one or two personal references. Two great maritime pioneers were sacrificed in the opening up of the East. John Davis, who sailed again in 1604 as pilot in an independent venture by Sir Edward Michelbourne, was killed, December 17, 1605, in an encounter with a Japanese junk off Bintang in the Straits of Malacca. William Baffin, who set sail in the Company's fleet under Captain Shillinge, February, 1620, died in January 1621, of a wound, received in a fight with the Portuguese in the Island of Kishm, south of Ormuz, and was buried there. The romantic story of William Adams has been retold by the aid of documentary evidence recently investigated. Arriving with the remnant of the Dutch fleet, of which, it will be remembered, he was pilot-major, on the coast of Japan in 1600, he first heard of the appearance of his countrymen in the Eastern Archipelago in 1611. In reply to a communication from him the Company sent an expedition to Japan, and in 1613 their ship *Clove*, under the command of

[1] "First Letter Book," p. 13.

Captain Saris, received a welcome which led to the establishment of the first English factory in the charge of Richard Cox or Cocks. Thus the English reached the furthest centre of importance in the far East within three and twenty years of the return of Ralph Fitch, the pioneer Englishman to the East; the first to tell his countrymen, from the evidence of his personal observation, of the wealth that lay under the rising sun.[1]

Another glimpse of Burma.

In no part of the British Empire in the East has the change of rule been more marked, or have the benefits thus conferred been more striking, than in Burma. Three centuries ago the whole of the fertile delta was laid waste, as the result of many years of war, conquest, and reconquest. The subsequent history of the country, from the sea, up the river valleys, to the mountains, was to a large extent a repetition of what had gone before, till we come to the romantic story of Alompra (Alaunghpra), the hunter from the woods, who filled the *rôle* of conqueror and king with considerable success and founded a dynasty. Our three Burmese wars of the present century culminated in the annexation of the upper and remaining portion of the country by proclamation on January 1, 1886, and the deportation of the last monarch, Thibaw, whose reign at Mandalay had been marked by the worst features of an Oriental despotism. The pacification of Burma, the advancement to its

[1] For interesting details concerning Adams, see Danvers's "Letters." The "Diary of Richard Cocks" has been edited for the Hakluyt Society by Sir E. Maunde Thompson.

present condition of contentment and prosperity, is a marvel of modern annexation. In spite of the disturbed condition of the upper country in 1886, with no governing class worthy of the name, with organised dacoity rampant in all directions, with the ever-threatening and lawless hill-tribes on the north, east, and west, and, above all, with the crudest notions of loyalty, confidence, or obedience among the masses of the people—notwithstanding this anarchical state of affairs which the monarchy, just removed, encouraged rather than suppressed, it was found possible in ten short years to remove the country, as a whole, from under the immediate supervision of the Indian Government. On May 1, 1897, Burma was erected into a Lieutenant-Governorship under Sir Frederick Fryer, who, it was pointed out at the time, thus had placed under his direct rule, aided by a Legislative Council, a country as large as France, including the two Savoy provinces and the island of Corsica. It is not necessary to make more than passing reference to the continued progress of Burma since that time, for the official statistics are easily accessible. It is sufficient to state that, in the returns for 1896–7, Rangoon (founded by Alompra) stood third in the list of the six most important ports of our Indian Empire. An interesting and vivid light was thrown upon the subject in a speech recently delivered by the Marquis of Dufferin and Ava, who was Viceroy of India at the time of the annexation, and whose title includes a name associated with the ancient glories of the Burmese Empire. He spoke of the Burmese as a people "so attractive, amiable, and intelligent," and described them as "the only nation among whom we were not only respected and honoured but obeyed, and whose religion was the purest outside Christianity."[1]

As to the future of Burma, it is well to bear in mind that she has, as next-door neighbour on the East, the vast empire of China. Soon after the annexation of 1885–6 the Government at Pekin set up, *inter alia*, an old and shadowy suzerainty, a claim which was met by a continuance of the decennial mission and the giving of presents. How far the final solution of the problem of the Far East may affect her future prosperity it would be out of place here to attempt to estimate, even on the basis, which is patent to all the world, of her redundancy of natural resources and the ample promise of her natural character.

Comparison and conclusion.

Without attributing too much to the results of the Fitch expedition, it may at least be claimed that the news that one solitary English traveller had passed and re-passed the mysterious portals of the East added fuel to the flame of adventure which burst forth as the result of the downfall of Spain as a sea-power. Lancaster began his first voyage to India, it has been pointed out, a few weeks before Fitch landed in London, but it is not improbable—though we have no actual evidence of the fact—that intelligence of his safety, with some account of his impressions of commercial prospects in the Indian seas, had reached England before him. He lingered awhile in Asia

[1] At the Burma Dinner held in London on June 16, 1898.

Minor, and Aleppo had been for some years a depôt for English trade. In any case he was in ample time to take an invaluable part in the first systematic movement which resulted in the formation of the first East India Company—he came back, in fact, as a practical merchant to point out, for the first time, what were the possibilities and probabilities of a prosperous trade in the distant Indies. If any single man ever acted successfully in spying out a great and wealthy region for the benefit of his countrymen, Ralph Fitch did it.

It is impossible to forget that the rise of the English in the East was accompanied by the incipient decay of the power ostensibly in possession. Historical authorities generally agree in ascribing the remarkably sudden fall of Portuguese influence abroad to the union under the Crown of Spain, and the complications that resulted with other European nations. But when the rival fleets of the Dutch and English appeared in Eastern waters the thorough rottenness of the Portuguese colonial system, to which some reference has been made in the preceding pages, became exposed, and, so far as they were concerned, the fight for supremacy was a short one. The contest for the crown of the East, however, did not end here. There were the Dutch, whose rise was more brilliant and whose fall was only less rapid and complete than was the case with the nation they displaced. Their disappearance as a potential factor in the East is one of the startling facts of modern history. Possessed of many qualities which go to make a great, progressive nation, sturdy, enterprising, industrious, Holland never secured a firm hold upon the immediate results of her conquests in this region, and the most valuable of her acquisitions were soon wrenched, or slipped, from her grasp. Hunter, limiting himself to what may be described as the local argument, puts the case in two sentences: "The fall of the Dutch colonial empire resulted from its short-sighted commercial policy. It was deliberately based upon a monopoly of the trade in spices, and remained from first to last destitute of sound economical principles." Taking a more general view of the question in a comparative sense, Professor Seeley, in the interesting lectures already mentioned, urges that both Portugal and Holland had too small a basis. Moreover, the latter country was involved in European wars, while England, on the other hand, was but slightly connected with the European system.

The fact remains that England, dating, as it were, from the enterprise of one of her typical sons, has become the heiress of the East. To enter upon a discussion of the question how she has retained and enlarged her hold would be a considerable undertaking. But of one thing we may boast, and that is, that in spite of one or two serious mistakes, she has solved the problem of colonial government. Knit by ties unknown to the Portuguese, for example, and flourishing under a commercial system which the Dutch never seemed to be able to understand, Great and Greater Britain together, in the East and in all parts of the world, have opened an entirely new volume in the common history of mankind.

INDEX

[*The names quoted are used by Ralph Fitch.*]

BOOKS FOR RECREATION AND STUDY

THE ADVENTURE SERIES

POPULAR RE-ISSUE.

Each large crown 8vo., fully illustrated. Popular re-issue, **3s. 6d.** *per vol.; in two styles of binding, viz., decorative cover, cut edges; and plain library style, untouched edges.*

1. **Adventures of a Younger Son.** By EDWARD J. TRELAWNEY. Introduction by EDWARD GARNETT.
2. **Madagascar;** or, Robert Drury's Journal during his Captivity on that Island. Preface and Notes by Captain S. P. OLIVER, R.A.
3. **Memoirs of the Extraordinary Military Career of John Shipp.**
4. **The Buccaneers and Marooners of America.** Edited and Illustrated by HOWARD PYLE.
5. **The Log of a Jack Tar:** Being the Life of James Choyce, Master Mariner. Edited by Commander V. LOVETT CAMERON.
6. **Ferdinand Mendez Pinto, the Portuguese Adventurer.** New Edition. Annotated by Prof. A. VAMBÉRY.
7. **Adventures of a Blockade Runner.** By WILLIAM WATSON. Illustrated by ARTHUR BYNG, R.N.
8. **The Life and Adventures of James Beckwourth.** Mountaineer, Scout, Pioneer, and Chief of Crow Nation Indians. Edited by CHAS. G. LELAND.
9. **A Particular Account of the European Military Adventurers of Hindustan.** Compiled by HENRY COMPTON.